Build Trust@ work:

Stop doing work you dislike with people you don't trust

By Dionne England

Build Trust@Work:
Stop doing work you dislike with people you don't trust

Copyright © 2022 Dionne England
First edition March 2022

No part of this publication may be reproduced, distributed or transmitted in any form or by any means, including photocopying, recording, or other electronic or mechanical methods, without the prior written permission of the AUTHOR, except in the case of brief quotations embodied in critical articles or reviews or other non-commercial uses permitted by copyright law. For permission, write to the author at contact@dionnethewriter.com.

Cover design by Lovely Studios

Author information: Dionne England

contact@dionnethewriter.com
www.dionnethewriter.com

ISBN Print Book - 978-1-7780768-0-0

Contents

Foreward: Trust, Air Quality and Celery?..7

PART 1 Let's talk about Trust@Work

Chapter 1: Losing Your Corporate Innocence 12

Chapter 2: Trust Doesn't Get the Respect It Deserves............................18

Chapter 3: High Trust Company Profile - Starbucks 34

Chapter 4: It's The HOW, Not The WHAT 38

Chapter 5: High Trust Company Profile - Zappos!...................................49

Chapter 6: It's Just Business?..56

Chapter 7: High Trust Company Profile Berkshire Hathaway 65

Chapter 8: Do Organizations need to be high trust to be successful? ...68

Chapter 9: High Trust Company Profile - Method...................................75

Chapter 10: What About Creating Shareholder Value?............................80

Chapter 11: High Trust Company Profile - Netflix 88

Chapter 12: Principles Over Profits 92

Chapter 13: High Trust Company Profile - Patagonia 101

Chapter 14: What Trust Is Not 105

Chapter 15: High Trust Company Profile - Salesforce 109

PART 2 What can managers do?

Chapter 16: Give trust first..114

Chapter 17: How Managers Can Foster Trust With Their Teams 117

PART 3 Show me the money

Chapter 18: How Trust Impacts the Bottom Line 154

Chapter 19: Are you Trustworthy? 170

Chapter 20: Who do you want to be? 173

This book is dedicated to my younger self who often felt like a misfit in the Corporate world. And, when her ideas were different from those around her, assumed she was wrong. Little did she know that one day she would be writing books about those experiences.

Foreward:
Trust, Air Quality and Celery?

When is the last time someone brought up the topic of the level of trust we have in our leaders and organizations in casual conversation? Probably just as often as they bring up the topics of the air we breathe and celery. When life is running as we expect, we take trust, our air quality, and celery for granted.

What about when things do not run as expected? What happens when we feel we can't trust our leaders to act with integrity and follow through on commitments? What happens when the quality of our air is at risk, and threatens to disrupt life as we know it for all species of life on earth? What happens when the price of an innocuous vegetable like celery skyrockets overnight?

When those things happen, we can speak of nothing else.

The quality of our air and sustainability of our environment is in crisis. Temperatures are rising globally, generating extreme weather systems including intense hurricane seasons, flooding, tornadoes in unexpected locations, and severe forest fires. Warming temperatures are destabilizing our ecosystem with glaciers melting and wildlife losing its regular food sources and habitat. Under stable conditions, discussions about the air we breathe are generally relegated to scientists or school children learning about the atmosphere. When things go sideways and the environment is in crisis, it dominates our daily conversations and news headlines.

I had a similar experience when it comes to routinely doing my groceries at the local grocery store. I can confidently confirm that I have never had a conversation about celery in my entire life. Sure, maybe it was mentioned while relaying the ingredients for a recipe, but that's about it. Celery is a boring vegetable. It's mostly water and barely has a taste. I was never a fan. Then 2019 happened. I'm an avid juicer so I regularly bought my $1.99 bunch of celery. To my horror, the price of celery went up to $5.99 overnight. That's crazy. A 300% price increase.[1]

Some weeks I would have to go to three or four grocery stores to find one that had celery in stalk, I mean stock. The 2019 growing season was unseasonably cold and rainy in California where we get the majority of our celery supply in my part of the world. Add to that a juice fad that had celery as its key ingredient. I am sure that I talked about celery every single day in 2019. Suddenly celery was trending on news feeds.

Trust is no different. For many of us, working with and for trustworthy team members and leaders is normal and expected. We expect that leadership commitments will be kept. We expect that our leaders will follow regulatory rules and the law. We trust that organizational rules and policies apply to everyone equally. We trust that when our leaders say that we, the employees, are their most valuable asset, they are being sincere.

When we feel we can't trust our business leaders, we can talk of little else.

My belief that trust is at the core of healthy, thriving organizations that provide a positive environment for employees to do their best work is what compelled me to write this book.

PART 1

LET'S TALK ABOUT TRUST@WORK

Chapter 1:
Losing Your Corporate Innocence

When did you lose your corporate innocence? I lost mine on a Tuesday afternoon in October, over a decade ago. I recall the day vividly. That morning, I put on my favourite navy-blue suit and made a mental note to lodge a complaint with my dry cleaner. This isn't the first time I put on an outfit, only to find the waistband was tighter than usual. The hips as well, if I were to be honest. I was convinced they must be shrinking my clothes.

The moment came at 2 PM on a particularly stressful day. The company I worked for at the time announced that it was laying off 15% of its staff, which included six people from my team. By 2 PM that afternoon, anyone whose jobs had been eliminated throughout the organization had left the building. They had been given the news by their manager, cleared out their desks and returned their laptops and pass cards. The senior team met with each department to impart some key corporate messages. They shared context for these layoffs, as well as provided support and encouragement after what would have been an emotionally charged day, even for those who were

Chapter 1: Losing Your Corporate Innocence

fortunate to keep their jobs. The leader that came to speak to my team was someone I had a good relationship with, spanning several years. I had a tremendous amount of respect for him. I considered him a mentor. I trusted him.

I realize many people would find it naïve that I would ever trust a "corporate executive." I could hear one of my good friends wryly saying, " trusting him was your first mistake". I understand that sentiment. Many corporate executives have worked hard throughout their careers to give us ample reason to distrust them. At that point in time, I was not yet a jaded corporate citizen. That would come later. (And, I am happy to say that after a stint of jaded cynicism lasting several years, I'm back to my default optimism.)

At the risk of sounding even more gullible, I'll add that trusting your leader or manager should be the norm. That's why I wrote this book. The fact that it's not is a sad testament to the crisis of trust in our corporate world today.

Let's go back to 2 PM on that transformational Tuesday. For the next events of that afternoon to make sense to you, I need to backtrack for a moment, and provide you with some additional context.

Two months earlier....

Two months before that fateful Tuesday, there was some turmoil in the organization as it was heavily fined by its regulator for not following the required due diligence with a very large client, who had since filed for bankruptcy. Subsequent to the bankruptcy filing, many unscrupulous business practices were uncovered, including activities that would have, and should have, been prevented if proper due diligence had been completed by our company. Other organizations were also implicated, however our organization played the largest role and accordingly, we incurred the largest fine.

This scandal dominated the media for a couple of weeks as details unfolded. The fine would have an impact on our financial results.

Fast forward to that Tuesday afternoon at 2 PM.

The leader arrived on our floor in an impeccable navy blue suit; clearly he got my memo that navy blue was the colour for the day. My team gathered in the center of the floor, and he acknowledged that it was a difficult day for everyone as colleagues left the organization. He shared it was challenging for him as well.

The moment of untruth

Then it happened. I know he was just following the carefully crafted script from the corporate communications team. He explained to my team that many people may speculate that these layoffs are a direct result of the regulatory fine the organization had to pay, and that this was an effort to cut costs to offset the cash outlay. He adamantly tried to assure us all that the two events were unrelated. These layoffs were a routine and prudent exercise that all organizations complete in order to right size ("right size" was a popular term during this era).

All I could think was, "are you kidding me?"

Analysts were speculating about what the organization would do to regain shareholder confidence. This was on the news, in the newspapers, on the business news networks. I saw and heard it with my own eyes and ears, and I suspected that other people in the room did too. This took place prior to our current "fake news" era, when most things you read and heard in the media was well researched and had credability.

Chapter 1: Losing Your Corporate Innocence

I felt that during this corporate pep talk, I was being asked to conveniently remove my brain from my head, put it in my desk drawer, and accept everything being said to me at face value.

I was surprised. I was insulted. I was confused and disappointed.

Whose brain child was this?

My mind began to wander, trying to make sense of things. I thought about the top floor of the skyscraper we called "head office." I wondered who had been the mastermind behind this idea to try and dupe everyone. Who said, "let's just say this has nothing to do with the regulatory fine. We'll then cascade this simple message throughout the organization from the executive team. If it comes from the executive team, everyone will believe it, right?"

Based on my knowledge of how large corporations work, I am confident a small army of communications specialists and lawyers would have pored over every word, comma, semi-colon and font choice. It would have needed the endorsement of the top-level leaders. I guess this was an example of group think in action. So, every single one of those individuals thought this was a good idea, and no one considered for a moment that this may possibly be one of the worst ideas ever? They were deploying a transparent lie. Upon reflection, I realized that due to the likely endorsement from key influencers and momentum that can happen in meetings, if someone had raised a dissenting opinion, it could have been a career limiting move for them.

In an instant, it was crystal clear to me that I couldn't trust anything being said by this man I respected. Not because he's a bad person; I'm confident he's a fine human being. I'm sure he returns his grocery cart to the receptacle in the parking lot, brakes for squirrels crossing the road and drinks eight glasses of water each day. But I could no longer trust him because he was allowing the company to dictate what he had to say, even if it means stretching the truth to the point that what he was saying was in a different area code from the truth.

That's the day I lost my corporate innocence.

I'm not innocent in this story. I had my own speaking notes as well, which I would use to reinforce the leader's message and tow the line. I imagine some of my team members had a similar feeling about me after this event. In fact, it may have been the point when they stopped trusting *me*.

This represented one of many moments in my corporate life where I felt like I was a polka dot in an industry of stripes. I felt my strong reaction to what I saw as utter bullshit was evidence that I wasn't corporate material. If I was, this would have been routine for me. I figured that I wasn't shrewd or sophisticated enough to know that this is just how things roll in big business sometimes. Expediency to get everyone back to work and sweep this ugliness away was the priority. Shut up and suck it up, or leave.

My team was a customer-facing team, so there was an additional layer to this farce for us. Client-facing teams were given additional speaking notes to use if a client asked questions about the layoffs, which had also received wide media coverage. Sure enough, a client questioned one of my team members about the layoffs. After carefully relaying the key messages to the client that the layoffs had nothing to do with the regulator fines and were rather, a routine exercise in "right-sizing," the client burst into laughter and said, compassionately, "I know they make you say that." Awesome.

Chapter 1: Losing Your Corporate Innocence

I will never know who the genius was behind this communication plan.

Not only did the leadership team erode the trust of employees, but the trust of clients as well. They also reinforced the widely accepted belief that is prevalent today—you can't trust corporations.

Chapter 2:
Trust Doesn't Get the Respect It Deserves

In business we often have a bias to those things that are easily measured. Sales? There's a line on the income statement to capture sales. Cost of raw goods? There's a line for that as well. Profit margin? I know very smart analysts who could whip together a dazzling spreadsheet with pivot tables, charts, and graphs that could break that information down for you by country, region, office, and even client. How much do we spend on employee salaries? There's a line for that as well.

There's no line on the spreadsheet that captures the level of trust within an organization. The level of trust between the leadership team and the rest of the employees in the organization. Trust between managers and their team members. The trust between the organization and its clients. There is no line on an income statement that captures trust. That's because it wouldn't be just one line. The truth is, trust influences almost every single line on those key financial statements. Later on in the chapter *How does trust impact the bottom line?*, I'll go into great detail of all the financial benefits that high trust organizations enjoy.

Chapter 2: Trust Doesn't Get the Respect It Deserves

Myth busting

MYTH: Profit maximization and trust building are conflicting strategies

First, let's address a common misconception that focusing on treating employees well and maximizing earnings are concepts that are in conflict with each other. As a profit-maximizing organization, increasing the bottom line is the primary goal and sometimes that means introducing changes that will piss off employees. We do whatever is required to maintain and improve our profitability and employees win by getting to keep their jobs. That's just life, right? Wrong.

The unalienable truth is that no company continues to exist and thrive if money coming in isn't greater than the money going out. That's just math. No one is going to purchase a mediocre product or service from you just because you're a good person and treat your employees well. **No one.**

You will notice that I profile seven high trust organizations throughout this book. Its noteworthy that that their financial performance is near or at the top of their industry. The myth I want to bust is the thought that being high trust and having strong business results are conflicting concepts. These companies are at the top of their game because building trust runs through their veins.

All of these organizations have had setbacks, including disappointing quarterly and annual returns. Most have had to lay staff off. Laying staff off, although unpleasant, does not erode the trust built with your employees. Trust is eroded when employees believe they are not being treated fairly. Trust is eroded when, as my Caribbean grandmother used to say, you're trying to give someone a "6" and tell them it's a "9." Trust is eroded when you lay off 15% of your employees to recoup from a large regulatory penalty and then tell your employees an entirely different story.

The reality is that when you decide you're going to be a high trust organization, you may need to pass on some short-term opportunities to make a financial quick win. You may need to fire a high performing sales person because their behaviour is not consistent with the corporate values and negatively impacts the company's reputation and employee morale. You may need to fire a big client who is not respectful of your team members and routinely makes unreasonable demands. You may incur additional expenses to find a new supplier for one of your products when you learn the current supplier's costs are low because their manufacturing process is damaging to the environment or has sub-standard safety measures in place to protect their employees.

High trust organizations don't view profitability as a short-term endeavor. They believe in the value of being high trust and know it's a long-term game. Foregoing some short-term wins that are at odds with their principles reinforces and builds their reputation as high trust. In the chapter ***Principles over Profits***, I share some examples where individuals and organizations took the more difficult road that aligned with their principles rather than taking the easy way out. I don't think we are ever truly considered high trust until we've been in one of these situations and demonstrated that we will stick to our principles.

MYTH: High trust has no tangible benefit for an organization

Here is a short summary of the value of being a high trust organization.

Chapter 2: Trust Doesn't Get the Respect It Deserves

Impact for Employees

When our employees realize that we, as leaders, are setting them up for success, genuinely have their back and are loyal to them, they are willing to go "over and above" to deliver for the organization. Employees are more engaged in high trust organizations and stay longer so you don't experience the disruption and astronomical costs associated with frequent turnover. Engaged employees with long tenure tend to be more knowledgeable, provide accurate information to clients and make fewer mistakes.

The primary purpose of the organization isn't to make employees feel loved and cherished. Organizations have all kinds of mandates. Some organizations strive to help their clients build wealth by providing creative, flexible and competitive financial products, services and strategies. Other organizations promise you they have the hottest, most stylish outfits that are good quality and reasonably priced. Your company may provide fast, reliable and high-quality maintenance and servicing for heating and air conditioning units. If these organizations plan to be around for the long term, they need to provide great value for their clients while also generating a profit. This is not a well-kept secret. Organizations need skilled employees in all of their roles, prudent financial management, a good strategy and talented managers to execute that strategy efficiently.

High trust organizations have figured out that we can treat our employees well while being efficient, innovative and profitable. More accurately, what they've actually figured out is that it's far easier to run a winning team when employees are engaged, loyal and committed to making the organization a success.

The footnote I will add here is that high trust organizations are rigorous about the employees they recruit and retain. We'll talk more about this in the chapter *Are you trustworthy?* Would a high trust organization want to hire you? In the company profile for Netflix, Zappos and Berkshire Hathaway, being rigorous about hiring trustworthy individuals is foundational for the sustainability of their empowering corporate cultures and their organization's superior results. Here I'll just state that in order for an organization to treat you with trust and provide you with the autonomy and empowerment to thrive, you must be trustworthy. Employees who seek to exploit the freedoms of empowering corporate cultures to benefit themselves at the expense of colleagues and the larger organization should be expediently shown the door.

Many large, bureaucratic corporations address the issue of untrustworthy employees by creating copious and restrictive policies and rules. They essentially create policies that cater to the lowest common denominator of their employee base. They then require managers to waste their time monitoring to ensure that everyone is following the rules, call out anyone who is offside while working through multiple layers of management for approvals for even the simplest requests. These excessive rules stifle your most effective employees feeling they are always being monitored. The managers who are now charged with monitoring aren't thrilled about it either as they're reduced to part-time babysitters.

High trust organizations respectfully yet efficiently show these low trust employees to the door and reject building bureaucracy and red tape to monitor folks who probably shouldn't be working there.

Chapter 2: Trust Doesn't Get the Respect It Deserves

Impact on Clients

Being high trust is a big win for clients. Clients get to speak to engaged, knowledgeable employees who give them accurate information. When clients call into your contact center, they rarely hear the recorded notice that wait times are longer than expected as you don't have a high absenteeism rate and most days you're running with a full ship. Clients have less reason to call your contact center as their products and services run as expected because you have a low defect rate. The end result is you have a happy client and happy clients tend to stick around longer than clients who are disappointed or frustrated.

We're used to hearing about the antics of low trust organizations

Unfortunately, we are used to hearing about the exploits of what can feel like an endless number of low trust organizations acting without a conscience to make a few extra dollars. A few of these examples from the past few years include:

- Volkswagen falsifying the emission tests of its cars during the period 2009-2015 to sell more cars under the guise of being environmentally friendly to gain market share.[1]
- The opportunist CEO, Martin Shkreil of Turing Pharmaceuticals raising the price of a life-saving drug 56x from $13.50 to $750 in an effort to turbo charge profits at the expense of the people who rely on the drug for their quality of life and in some cases, to stay alive. The drug became unaffordable overnight and alternatives were significantly less effective.[2]
- In April 2017, United Airlines ordered security personnel to drag passenger Dr. David Dao off an overbooked

flight at O'Hare's airport in Chicago. The scene was caught on video and went viral. Dr. Dao suffered a concussion, broken nose and lost two teeth in the unfortunate episode.[3]
- Wells Fargo applied pressure to their frontline teams to attain unreasonable sales targets. Bank executives eventually admitted to regulators that the sales targets were unrealistic. In order to meet these sales targets frontline teams started an elaborate plan to falsify additional client accounts. They were effectively defrauding their clients while the executives looked in the other direction, happy with the new revenue.[4]

Sadly, I could have written a novel to document all of the corporate scandals that took place in just the last 10 years; multiple volumes if I included the lesser known scandals that didn't make it into the national news headlines.

In this book, I don't tackle the flagrant assaults on our collective sense of integrity that I noted above. We leave the resolution of those scandals to a combination of the judicial process, regulatory fines, public exposure….and hopefully therapy and introspection.

This is why we hear things like, "you can't trust a profit-driven organization to do the right thing." My hope with this book is that I will share encouraging stories about some incredible organizations that are committed to operating with high trust while also dominating their industry.

Hope is on the horizon

There are encouraging signs if we recognize them. In 2021, US President Joe Biden stated that he will fire on the spot

Chapter 2: Trust Doesn't Get the Respect It Deserves

anyone seen to be disrespectful to colleagues. Is this just the kind grandfather-in-chief having a "Kumbaya moment" and asking everyone to play nice? Not at all. He understands that respect is fundamental for building a safe and trusting work environment. Respect creates safety for team members to engage in heated and spirited debates on the best way forward and hopefully making a path for the best option to make itself known. Respectful interactions build trust and creates an environment that makes it easier for people to do their best work. We need to be able to offer our work colleagues the same level of respect that is expected of students in any Grade 2 classroom.

Additionally, there is greater transparency, wanted or not, through social media. The hypocrisy of espousing the virtues of respect and trust publicly while practicing the opposite behind closed doors is easily exposed.

Its difficult to conceal shady corporate behaviour long term

Uber became the poster child in 2017 for what can happen when there's a corporate culture of dishonesty and distrust. All of the examples I've listed below were sourced from the article by Julia Carrie and Sam Morris in the Guardian publication (www.theguardian.com) entitled ***Collision course: Uber's terrible 2017.*** Get comfortable as 2017 was an eventful year for Uber and the list of their transgressions is pretty long.

The year 2017 started for Uber by paying out $20 million in a settlement based on a case brought against them that they misled drivers about their potential earning opportunity with the company. In that same month, taxi drivers in New York City went on a one hour strike to protest the government's implementation of a travel ban. On the night of the taxi driver strike, Uber put out an announcement that they would not impose surge pricing. Uber insists they were simply saying they wouldn't impose the higher fares that would naturally kick in when demand out paces the supply for transportation and therefore they would forego the higher profit margins they would naturally experience during a taxi strike. Consumers interpreted Uber's announcement differently, believing that Uber was trying to garner extra business, exploiting the taxi strike. In the chapter ***How trust impacts the bottom line***, I share the value of a company building goodwill with the marketplace. When you have a long track record of acting with integrity, when there are missteps or misunderstandings, customers are inclined to give you the benefit of the doubt. Uber's goodwill jar was completely empty. Their announcement outraged many customers and was the catalyst for the #deleteuber to trend on social media resulting in thousands of customers requesting to delete their Uber accounts.

It was only the second month of 2017 when Uber was hit again when a former engineer with the company, Susan Fowler, published a piece outlining the rampant sexual harassment and gender discrimination that she believed was prevalent within the organization. Susan's public allegations lead to an internal investigation and later in the year, several employees were fired for sexual misconduct on the job. But February wasn't over yet. In February, Waymo, Google's self-driving car company, sued Uber for plotting to steal key intellectual property pertaining to self-driving technology.

In March, then CEO, Travis Kalanick is caught on video verbally abusing an Uber driver. He subsequently issued a formal apology to the driver. Also in March the Uber executive team was reported to have visited an escort- karaoke bar in Seoul,

Chapter 2: Trust Doesn't Get the Respect It Deserves

South Korea. March also saw the revelation that Uber had deployed a tool called "Greyball" which allowed Uber to deceive local authorities making it appear they were following local regulations when they were not. Uber wrapped up March by publishing a diversity report which showed a stark absence of diversity in their workforce with the vast majority of their workforce being white and male.

In April, it was revealed that Uber has a secret program called "Hell" which spied on its competitor Lyft. It was also revealed that Uber was breaking Apple's privacy rules with its iOS application compelling Tim Cook, CEO of Apple to personally address the issue with Kalanick.

In May Uber admitted that they have been underpaying New York City drivers which cumulatively short changed them a total of tens of millions of dollars in earnings.

In June, a top executive admits that he stole the medical records of a passenger who was raped by an Uber driver. Her medical records were stolen in an effort to undermine the credibility of her allegations. In June, Kalanick finally submitted to pressures from major investors to step down as CEO.

In August, Uber rented cars to drivers in Singapore despite knowing that the cars in question had been recalled by the manufacturer due to safety issues.

In September Uber loses its license to operate in London, England due to their poor corporate governance.

In November it was revealed that Uber suffered a data breach in 2016 exposing the data of 57 million customers and drivers. Uber paid a ransom to have the data destroyed and the breach to remain confidential.

It appears that karma was Uber's constant companion in 2017. You may be thinking that despite these brazen breaches of trust, Uber is a wildly successful organization adding a new verb to our vocabulary. Everyone knows what you mean when you say you're going to "uber it". Uber has been an recognized as an iconic brand with substantial growth and potential. As a result, Uber has attracted massive amounts of capital investment over the years. It should be noted, however, that since its founding in 2009, 2021 was the first year where Uber had a profitable quarter. There are a number of factors within its business model that has made it challenging to turn a profit. I'm not a financial analyst however I will go out on a limb and assert that paying out millions of dollars to settle disputes doesn't help its profitability. Additionally, the "#deleteuber" movement saw the loss of thousands of customer accounts. I don't think these former customers decided to embrace pedestrian life but rather, signed up with one of Uber's competitors. Then there's the time, money and resources dedicated to the multiple suits and investigations which would distract the leadership of the organization. Uber has been temporarily banned from operating in a few major cities, with London, England being just one. Then regulators and local governments would likely exercise extra scrutiny with Uber given its track record for deceit.

Uber lost close to 40% of its market value as a result of these and other scandals[5].

Some organizations don't quite understand the concept of trust

I was shocked when watching the Feb 22, 2021 episode of ***Last Week Tonight with John Oliver*** (one of my all-time favourite shows), where John documented the appalling treatment of Tyson Food employees during the Coronavirus pandemic in 2020. Tyson's meatpacking plant in Waterloo, Iowa was

Chapter 2: Trust Doesn't Get the Respect It Deserves

ordered to be closed in April of 2020 after an inspection by the County Sheriff, Tony Thompson. Sheriff Thompson was deeply disturbed by the working conditions he observed given the growing pandemic. The health measures required to minimize the spread were being ignored. Tyson refused to close and subsequently, over 1,000 employees were infected at that specific plant. There's a lawsuit in progress by the son of one of the employees who contracted the virus and subsequently died. It was a sad and shocking story, but it gets worse. There's documented evidence that the managers at the Waterloo Tyson plant created a betting pool where they wagered on who would be the next employee to get infected with COVID-19.[6] The words callous and obscene come to my mind.

Let's juxtapose that story with Tyson Foods promotional videos where they describe their employees as family. They profess their employees are their most valuable asset and everyone on the team is focused on protecting each other. It's a heart-warming video and vividly underlines my argument that, you just can't fake trust.

Leadership under the microscope

In Canada, we have an investigation underway examining the management practices in the former Governor General's office. A workplace review conducted by a consulting firm, uncovered substantial allegations raised by 92 individuals describing acts of bullying and disrespect that generated tears in some and resignation letters in others. If you're like me and you've worked for more than a handful of years, you've undoubtedly done some time in a toxic work environment for a few weeks or possibly several years. Most of the individuals fostering these toxic environments are never reported and so the behaviour persists.

It's a courageous act for staff to come forward with these types of allegations against their leader. The internal channels to report these issues often can't be trusted to be objective and unfortunately in many cases employees fear their allegations will backfire on them and be channeled right back to the leader in question. It can be career limiting to raise concerns about your leader. Although it's illegal to take recourse on an employee for raising a complaint, there are many subtle ways that revenge can be delivered especially in a low trust environment that likely lacks the leadership integrity to ensure there is no recourse.

Consider that in the case of the Canadian Governor General's office, of the 92 individuals who spoke confidentially during the workplace review, not a single individual felt comfortable to raise a complaint through the multiple internal channels that were available to them over the 4-year period in question. Yet, the infractions were egregious enough to trigger the immediate resignation of the Governor General. As I listened to news reports and first-hand testimonials by those who worked there, I was struck by how so much of this situation mirrors what happens today in many organizations.

Despite the pain this undoubtedly caused the staff of the Governor General's office, I am hopeful that the high-profile probe will act as a signal, at least for Canadian companies, about the consequences of accommodating toxic work environments. A strong message that this is not okay. It is anticipated that there will be remedies prescribed to those negatively impacted. I am very curious to learn about the recommendations that will surface for those internal channels including

Chapter 2: Trust Doesn't Get the Respect It Deserves

the HR department. I trust this will spawn some hard realities about why employees didn't trust the formal channels. People chose to resign or go on short-term leave from their positions rather than file a grievance through HR.

In this book, I will outline the value of trust between an organization and its employees, its clients, and the communities they serve. I'll highlight some of the well-intentioned missteps some corporations make in an effort to foster trust when they don't fundamentally understand or value trust. I'll show the competitive advantage enjoyed by the high trust organizations. I hope you especially enjoy the company profiles found throughout this book where we find models of successful organizations committed to maintaining high trust, empowering cultures as a long term business strategy. I hope these profiles are encouraging, melt some cynicism and inspires hope that this trend of organizations seeking to genuinely build trust with its stakeholders will grow.

Trust has to grow if organizations intend to remain competitive. Trust will increasingly be a competitive advantage. The cost of doing business for high trust organizations is lower than that of their lower trust peers. Finally, employee expectations are changing. We didn't survive through a once-in-a-lifetime pandemic to continue to endure unnecessary stress and anxiety in low trust, toxic work environments. Employees are seeking more fulfillment and humanity in their workplaces.

Who am I speaking to in this book?

In this book, I speak primarily to middle managers. I adore middle managers. Much like trust, I also don't think middle managers get the love and respect that they deserve. Middle management is a challenge. We are infatuated with the Chiefs:

the Chief Executive Officer, the Chief Finance Officer, the Chief Technology Officer, the Chief Information Officer, and the list goes on for days. These folks sit at the top of the organization. They design and champion the corporate strategy. But once that corporate strategy is established, it's left to the middle managers to operationalize it through the organization to turn the strategy into results.

One of my favourite sayings is that a mediocre strategy executed expertly will always outperform a brilliant strategy poorly executed. A corporate strategy will thrive or die with middle management.

Weak middle managers often lack the leadership skills to motivate and lead their team towards success. As a result, the strategy is never fully implemented and doesn't render the desired results.

Then there are the great middle managers. They wear many hats and do it all so well. Where the leadership team effectively communicates the what, why, who, where and when of the strategy from the top of the organization to the most junior roles, middle managers can then assume their role to reinforce the strategy and help everyone on their team understand their specific role. Where the leadership team isn't as effective as communicators, middle managers are also charged with selling the dream to their teams and ensuring everyone understands the strategy.

Middle managers are coaches, monitors, problem solvers, production drivers, communicators, mediators, motivators and champions. They also hold their colleagues and team members accountable and may be part time babysitters and possibly therapists. When required, they recruit for vacant positions and foster engagement off the side of their desk.

Chapter 2: Trust Doesn't Get the Respect It Deserves

Middle managers wear many hats. I provide strategies, tactics, tools and hacks for middle managers to foster high trust among their teams making it easier for them to achieve success with less effort.

Chapter 3:
High Trust Company Profile - Starbucks

Starbucks has transformed the coffee experience for millions of people around the world. In his book ***Onward***, Howard Schultz, the founder of Starbucks shares the story of when he fell in love with the coffee experience on a business trip in Milan. Howard originally worked for a small coffee company named "Starbucks" which he later bought and grew into the international coffee company we know today. He talks about the enchanting scene he experienced in these Italian coffee houses. The warmth of the barrista and the drama of the coffee making process. The smell. The superior taste of the coffee. But more than anything else, what struck him was the collegial feeling among the patrons and the staff. He described that in each coffee bar he visited he "felt the hum of community".[1]

It took years but Schultz was on a mission to bring that vibe to his coffee customers in the US. Over the years, Starbucks has had phenomenal success with legions of loyal customers around the world. They've also had some missteps, challenges and setbacks. Through the years, Starbucks has held tight to its core values. It's more than coffee. It's about quality products.

Chapter 3: High Trust Company Profile - Starbucks

It's about lifestyle. It's about community. That's the experience I have when I place my order with a friendly barista who is usually up for small banter that doesn't sound like it was memorized from a customer service script. Starbucks has also chosen to have a deeper connection with the communities where its coffee houses are located. After announcing one of the unfortunate rounds of store closures there were demonstrations in some communities with customers advocating to keep their local Starbucks open. It's more than just coffee.

What does Starbucks do?

Starbucks describes itself as offering "more than just coffee and tea"[2] They are a chain of coffeehouses that sells food and beverages at locations throughout the world.

What is their position within the industry?

Starbucks has the largest marketshare for coffee houses in the US representing 40% of the US market.[3]

Why do we trust them – Reason #1

Meaningful response to organizational issues – Actions match words

In April of 2018 there was an unfortunate incident at a Starbucks store in Philadelphia. Two African American men walked into the City Center Starbucks in downtown Philadelphia. They asked to use the washroom and were declined by staff as they didn't purchase anything. After the two men sat down, waiting for another colleague who was meeting them at Starbucks, the staff member called the police reporting that the gentlemen were trespassing. The police showed up and after some discussion, the men were lead out of the Starbucks in handcuffs and arrested.[4]

The Starbucks CEO condemned the incident on social media the same day with a commitment that Starbucks will learn and grow from this unfortunate experience. Starbucks then followed through on their commitment. They closed all of their stores for an afternoon to run all of their employees through a training program. In an act of transparency, Starbucks made all the training material and leadership videos available to the public. Starbucks leadership remained consistent with their values and had a thoughtful, meaningful response to a very unfortunate incident.[5]

Why do we trust them – Reason #2

Tangible commitment to having a diverse workforce

Starbucks's workforce is quite diverse comprising of 69% women and 47% BIPOC.[6] Through their initiative "Commitment to Opportunity for Youth," they actively hire 16-24 year olds who are not working or in school. Starbucks has recruited 50 other businesses to join this initiative, which allowed them to exceed their goal to hire 100,000 youth over a 3-year period. In partnership with Arizona State University, Starbucks also offers university education at minimal personal cost to youth.[7]

Why do we trust them – Reason #3

Commitment to providing health care benefits to employees

Howard Schultz returned to rescue Starbucks in 2008 after their performance declined due to over-expansion and other leadership decisions that didn't align with corporate values. At

Chapter 3: High Trust Company Profile - Starbucks

the time, Schultz came under pressure from shareholders to cut health care benefits for employees. Starbucks spends more on health care than it does on coffee. One investor counselled Schultz that the 2008 recession would be the perfect scapegoat to give him a good cover to cut employee benefits. Schultz remained true to the company's commitment to provide health care benefits to its employees and advised the investor, instead, that if they felt strongly that health care benefits should be cut, perhaps they should sell their Starbucks shares and invest in a company that matched their philosophy.[8]

Chapter 4:
It's The HOW, Not The WHAT

Being a high trust organization does not make you immune to the challenging times that inevitably show up. Challenging times are fertile ground to deepen the level of trust an organization has with its stakeholders.

Franklin Delano Roosevelt knew a lot about challenging times. He was the US President in the 1930's and had to lead the country through the Great Depression. He reminds us that "a smooth sea never made a skilled sailor."[1]

When faced with uncertainty and the best next step is unclear or you're under pressure to perform, it can be tempting to abandon our core values, thinking it's just temporary until things turn around. We may be eager to take a more expedient action even if it alienates a stakeholder like a colleague, employees, our customers or our vendors.

All companies encounter uncertainty and challenges regardless of how big and seemingly successful they are. Zappos! has an iconic reputation for being an inspiring place to work, and they've had to lay off staff. Starbucks turns 50 in 2021 and over the years, they've had layoffs and store closings as they

Chapter 4: It's The HOW, Not The WHAT

navigated growth, contraction, and marketplace changes. In the company profiles in this book, you'll see that these difficult moments were managed in a manner that remained true to the organization's core values. These companies haven't maintained their high trust work environment despite these challenging times. They've maintained their high trust work environment because of the way in which they conducted themselves during these difficult periods. Often, it wasn't pretty and they made some missteps but they were deeply thoughtful, transparent, and courageous. They put one foot in front of the other each day and made the best decisions they could while holding tightly to their core values even when it didn't appear that in the short run those values were serving them well. They maintained a long term perspective.

The point here is not what they needed to do. At some point, most companies need to raise prices, lay off staff, close some manufacturing or retail outlets, relocate operations a significant distance away, outsource or automate certain functions. The salient point is that although all organizations may encounter similar challenges over time, **HOW** the leadership team chooses to navigate these challenges and **HOW** they work with their employees, clients, vendors and other stakeholders through it will make all the difference in the world.

Let's take a look at layoffs and data breaches to illustrate the point that how we manage challenges makes all the difference. Both of these events are painful and unfortunate and often breed distrust among employees and/or customers. Let's see how an organization can take these bad situations and improve it by their response.

Most companies get layoffs all wrong

This is probably one of the most difficult situations from an employee's perspective, especially when the need for the layoffs was due to a miscalculation or poor planning by the leadership team. As humans, at times we like to motor through difficult life experiences, business or personal, to get to the other side of it as quickly as possible. I've witnessed this mindset at work on multiple occasions with layoffs. The rationale is to rip off the bandage and get the remaining employees re-focused and back on track as quickly as possible. No need to wallow in grief and sadness.

On the day that employees are to be informed of the layoffs, an elaborate HR operation is executed with those employees targeted to leave the organization often ushered into a room a few floors away from their regular work environment, to meet with a complete stranger from an outsourcing company or an HR team member they probably have had limited exposure to in the past. This individual will then relay that their job is no longer required. The departing employees are told the layoffs "aren't personal" and definitely not a reflection on their performance but rather, a case of the proverbial "shit happens." This stranger, or near stranger, genuinely exhibits the technical ingredients of compassion like addressing the fact that "I know this is difficult to hear" and "we realize you will need some time to digest this information", but, as these newly unemployed individuals have no real relationship with this individual, there's only so much genuine comfort that can be felt from these words. Counsellors are always on hand should someone get overly emotional. Packages are available for the individuals to read through their options and outplacement support. Sometimes individuals are allowed back to their

Chapter 4: It's The HOW, Not The WHAT

desk, escorted, in the awkward act of cleaning out their critical personal belongings. Sometimes a stranger, manager or co-worker is sent to their desk. Passcards are confiscated and the individuals in question leave the building never to return.

Back in the office, those employees who remain may have witnessed some of the awkward desk clearings and word is already spreading throughout the organization that something is going down. It's not difficult to decipher what's going on when your once bubbly co-worker marches to their desk with an escort, avoids eye contact with you, clears out some personal items, grabs their coat, and walks out.

The remaining group of employees are assembled once all employees have left the premises and provided with a carefully scripted speech about why there's a need for reducing the size of the workforce. If there's any plausible argument to say that its marketplace pressures, that is surely going to be the selected reason. There is always a sincere sentence to thank those that left for the "invaluable contribution they have made to our organization." We are assured our former colleagues are well taken care of and have an abundance of support as they transition into a new bright opportunity someplace else.

What follows in the presentation is often a quick pivot to focus on the future. We are given a rousing motivational speech about how well this positions us for the future and we should be encouraged by all the great successes we will have going forward. The employees who remain are told how valuable they are. They are essentially encouraged to shake off the events of the day and move on. Find the silver lining. Look on the bright side. See the opportunity in this challenging time.

Now, there are some very practical reasons for executing restructuring efforts in this manner. Employees who are just learning that they're being laid off can become quite emotional. It's often more compassionate for them to be able to experience that away from their team. They may prefer for someone else to collect their belongings from their desk so they don't need to face their colleagues in the moment while they are still digesting what's going on.

In some extreme situations, employees exiting the company get angry. They lash out and try to cause some form of harm to the organization in an effort to seek revenge on their perceived rejection by the organization. Perhaps lashing out comes in the form of spreading negativity amongst the remaining employees letting them know this could happen to them as well and the company doesn't give a fuck about them. Maybe it's sending confidential files to their home email with malicious intent. Whatever they choose to do, it's in the organization's best interest to handle the layoffs in a manner that limits the opportunity for these kinds of destructive acts to occur. I understand the rationale behind designing such a regimented approach to exiting employees from the company.

The challenge is that this approach also erodes trust and morale in those exiting the organization as well as those staying.

Those leaving are left feeling:
- Undervalued as they are now spending their last hour with the organization with strangers, who speak using empty platitudes
- Untrustworthy as they're often escorted first to their desk then out of the building like a trespasser

Those employees remaining are left feeling:
- Vulnerable at the thought that they could be next should circumstances call for further reductions in staff

Chapter 4: It's The HOW, Not The WHAT

- Sad as they empathize with their colleagues leaving the organization and imagine how difficult that must be
- Anxious as they wonder how they will manage the team's heavy workload with less people. Surely the work isn't exiting the building with their former colleagues.

If it's perceived that the true fault was a management error in decision-making, the lack of accountability by the leadership team for that error breeds distrust and resentment.

Suggestions on making layoffs a little less awful

I won't pretend that there's actually a win-win scenario with layoffs. I do believe that there are ways that are better than others. Here are a few ideas.

Be honest about the reason behind the layoff. This is not the time for a marketing spin. If the reason for the layoffs is that the company expanded too quickly, then say so. Even if you pull off a marketing spin internally, trust that financial analysts and the media will be forthcoming on what it believes triggered the restructuring. Not only will employees lose trust in you if they find out you lied to them, they will also resent you for assuming they were naïve enough to believe your spin. I can personally attest to this truth. You may have a larger cubicle, larger salary and more influence, but your employees are the heart and soul of your organization. In many cases, they are the face and voice of your organization for your customers. Show them the respect they deserve by being transparent with them.

Be accountable. If layoffs are the result of a company misstep, take accountability as a company in the same manner we expect employees to take accountability for their mistakes.

Explain how it happened and most importantly, share what the company will do moving forward to ensure the same mistake is not repeated. Layoffs are difficult for those left behind as well as those who exit the organization so provide them with assurances that the organization takes this step seriously and will do whatever they can to avoid a repeat. There are no guarantees, but the commitment of leadership to avoid the circumstances that made these layoffs necessary is helpful. Some CEOs make commitments, like promising no further layoffs for at least the next 12 months. If that's a promise you can keep, it will help to create some stability and show your commitment to your team. Unfortunately, some organizations trigger layoffs as a tool to ensure the business meets its financial goals. Despite the heartfelt words on the day of the layoffs, some organizations can be indifferent to layoffs, shrugging them off with a sense of "it's just business." Some organizations use layoffs as a tool to improve the financial performance and view it no differently than process re-engineering.

Be candid and answer questions honestly. Anticipate key questions and answer them candidly by sharing as much as is possible. Anticipate these types of questions on your team's mind:

- Why did this happen?
- Other than these layoffs, will there be any other impacts?
- Do you anticipate more layoffs?
- How will we maintain our workload with a smaller team?

Managers should layoff their employees themselves, in person if possible – for the same reasons we don't break up with our partner by text, terminating an employee in person

Chapter 4: It's The HOW, Not The WHAT

is always the preference. Barring a situation which prevents an in-person meeting, every effort should be made for an in-person discussion with a video conference being the next best, but clearly inferior, option. Giving someone your time and enduring the difficult conversation is an unspoken message that shows that the employee is important enough to warrant the effort and sends a message to others.

Treat the individual with the respect they deserve for the contribution they have made to the organization. Be sincere and empathetic, and let them feel badly in the moment if that's what happens. I don't think it's possible to make it a good day, unless the individual was actually hoping for this outcome, but you can take a terrible moment and make it a little less terrible.

Move on but show some love. When we've worked closely with co-workers, particularly over years, they feel like family. They are our work family. Layoffs can feel like losing a part of your family. There's no value in wallowing in sadness and loss for weeks or even months while playing Adele on repeat. There's a better solution between never-ending grief and ripping off the bandage, shaking it off, and moving on in the span of an afternoon. The way you treat exiting employees sends loud cues to the remaining employees about their value. They're fully aware that it could have been them. It informs whether they truly believe the message at the next Employee Appreciation event.

In reality, this message is less about the words stated on this particular afternoon and more about how the organization operates daily. If you're a high trust organization and most employees believe this is an unfortunate event but the leadership team is a capable group of individuals who are benevolent and act with integrity, this shouldn't be an issue.

How can an organization navigate a data breach with integrity?

Organizations have large amounts of its data stored digitally. Our customers send us an increasing amount of data digitally, and the 2020 pandemic pushed a rapid adoption of remote mediums from even the most resistant technophobes. Cybersecurity is a growing priority for organizations as cyber criminals diligently poke and prod to uncover weaknesses in a company's data security. What that means for me is that I have so many complex passwords with numbers, letters, upper case, lower case, special characters and acronyms that I am actually the main person I am protecting my data from. I'm constantly having to click on "forgot password" only to be prodded to create another complex combination of characters which I will soon forget.

A cybersecurity leak is never good news for an organization. Mistakes happen, but **HOW** we choose to handle it makes all the difference and demonstrates to our stakeholders if they were wise in putting their trust in us.

Let's take a look at how MyHeritage.com expertly managed a data breach in 2018 when more than 92,000 client email addresses were leaked. MyHeritage is a genealogy company that allows people to trace their family roots online and provide details of family lines. Using DNA kits, customers add to MyHeritage's pool of DNA data which further assists users in connecting with family members around the world.

A leak of your email address may seem relatively harmless. What are they going to do? Flood my inbox with chain letters or videos of cats? Probably not, but you might receive phishing emails to try to dupe you into disclosing passwords to other

Chapter 4: It's The HOW, Not The WHAT

platforms, such as online banking, where far more damage can be done.

Unfortunately, we are used to seeing most companies trip themselves up when issues like data breaches happen. They get defensive and essentially focus on covering their corporate ass as the primary concern. While deciding on a strategy forward, days of silence pass with trite statements if any at all, making the bad situation worse due to the poor response.

MyHeritage, however, has received significant praise across the business world on how well they managed this unfortunate situation. Here are some key strategies they employed:

Timely transparent communication

MyHeritage reported the breach the day they became aware of it. They provided a detailed breakdown of the situation, and advised clients of how and when they would share further details with them. Speed is very important, as the faster customers are aware, the faster both the company and customers can follow the risk mitigation actions and the higher the likelihood that they can protect themselves before further damage is done by the hackers.

Put customers first

The focus for MyHeritage was to inform their customers to ensure they understood the potential impact this breech could have for them and provide them with clear, concise instructions on how they can protect themselves and limit further unwanted data exposure. They immediately set up a phone and email hotline for clients to provide 24-hour access to staff who could answer any questions they had. MyHeritage understood this was not a moment to be defensive and focus internally on the company. They understood clearly that their primary accountability was to their customers, who could potentially be personally impacted by this breach. They needed to provide them with as much information and useful guidance as possible.

I'm sure if MyHeritage could turn back time they would intervene to prevent the breach. As that's not one of the options that was available to them, they took the next best option to act as expediently and transparently as possible to protect their clients, mitigate the impact of the breach, and put stronger safeguards in place.

Rather than just talking about how they put their customers first, they took actions to put their customers' needs first.

Chapter 5:
High Trust Company Profile - Zappos!

I'm convinced I was destined to visit Zappos!. Those who know me, know that I'm a huge book nerd. It was 2010 and I was in desperate search for a new book to read on Audible as my commute at the time included a long stretch of construction making my drive longer than I thought was reasonable. ***Delivering Happiness*** by Tony Hsieh popped up as a recommended book based on my past reading choices. I remember thinking that it sounded so corny but I reluctantly started reading it. Amazon's algorithm knows my reading taste better than most people I know. All I can say is thank goodness for that construction to give me the extra time I needed to get through that book in just a few days. I absolutely fell in love with the book and Tony's story. Sadly Tony passed away in 2020 far too soon. He was a business visionary.

There's more to my story. I was finishing up the last chapter of ***Delivering Happiness*** on a Thursday morning and at the end of the book Tony invites people to visit Zappos! head office anytime they're in Las Vegas. Serendipitously, I was going to Las Vegas for the very first time the very next day. I ran into the office and called the number provided in the book and true to his word, someone at Zappos! booked me in for a company tour four days later on Monday.

That Monday they picked us up in the complimentary Zappos! shuttle at our hotel in Las Vegas and took us to their head office where we were greeted by warm and enthusiastic team members. The tour was great. The pride and energy of the employees is tangible. At the end of the tour, they offered us a free inspiring business book to help spread the message of how effective, successful and fulfilling a positive, empowered, inspiring culture can be. They are obsessed with their clients, kindness, having fun and working hard. I've been back to the head office and each time I visit I learn something new and walk away with tremendous hope. Zappos! is a live case study demonstrating that a high trust work environment where people feel comfortable being themselves while also knocking sales results out the door is the best way to do business.

What does Zappos! do?

Zappos! Is an online shoe and clothing retailer that sold a portion of its ownership to Amazon in 2009. If you check out their website Zappos! would have you know that they actually live and deliver WOW.

What is their position within the industry?

Tony Hseih launched Zappos! August of 1999 with a personal investment of $500,000 and sold it to Amazon Nov 2009, 10 years later for $1.2 billion.[1] Zappos! does not disclose its financials so more current financial data is not available.

Chapter 5: High Trust Company Profile - Zappos!

Why do we trust them – Reason #1
Commitment to hiring only individuals who will support their corporate culture and "wow" their customers

High trust organizations are able to empower their employees because they make sure they have the "right people on the bus". In the book *Good to Great* which is a classic that every manager should read, Jim Collins explains that we focus first on "who" then on "what". "Get the right people in the right seats on the bus" meaning that you should focus on hiring the right people and putting them in the right roles.

Zappos! is intentional in recruiting and hiring team members who will support their culture and be committed to "delivering wow" for their clients. Candidates apply online and are engaged by the recruitment team at Zappos! through video calls and online chats. Those candidates who are brought into head office for an interview are observed by the wide cross section of the Zappos! team, not just the interviewers. For example, candidates who flying in from another part of the country for the interview will be picked up at the airport by Zappos! staff and brought to head office. From the time the candidate gets in the Zappos! van, their behaviour is being observed. It's critical at Zappos! that team members demonstrate a high level of respect for others, trustworthiness and kindness.

If the candidate is hired, they participate in a four-week training program. At the end of that program, Zappos! offers candidates $2,000 to leave if they believe that Zappos is not the right fit for them. Zappos! reports that 2-3% of candidates take this offer and leave the organization. Amazon adopted this practice when they acquired Zappos![2]

If you've ever experienced having to "performance manage" employees who fall short of performance targets, aren't motivated, and/or demonstrate behaviour that is at odds with the organization's values, you know how tedious and time-consuming this process can be. It may end with the employee being terminated from the organization once the full remediation process is completed. The cost to the organization in terms of the time expended by the managers to manage the performance of team members underperforming, the lost opportunity as managers are not doing other more valuable activities, and the potentially negative impact this employee is having on the performance and the morale of other team members is exponentially higher than $2,000. This is a brilliant strategy by Zappos! to ensure that the candidates they hire are passionate about the company mandate and truly want to be there.[3] As a result of this hiring practice, Zappos! minimizes the instance of onboarding folks who are just along for the ride and happy to see how they can personally benefit from the empowered, autonomous work environment that Zappos! provides. Empowered, autonomous work environments with minimal rules and policies similar to Zappos! is only sustainable over time with trustworthy employees who respect and appreciate the environment they work in and reciprocate by doing their best work. Untrustworthy team members focused primarily on how the work environment can benefit them personally erodes the culture and, in worst case scenarios requires management to introduce draconian rules to control these low trust employees. It also unnecessarily occupies managers time who now have to babysit these employees.

Chapter 5: High Trust Company Profile - Zappos!

Why do we trust them – Reason #2
Commitment to over-the-top customer service

Zappos! doesn't employ scripts for their client loyalty officers. They prefer that their teams engage authentically with clients and make a real connection. Call times aren't monitored. The focus is to connect and resolve the client's inquiry and of course, wow them. There is no upselling at Zappos!. They see the upselling strategy as a customer irritant that works in the favour of the company but not the customer. Finally, stories are celebrated where team members go over and above to demonstrate they care. There are endless anecdotes about team members extending the standard return policy to accommodate a client who returned a product late because of a death in the family or some other impactful life event. They've sent a replacement product overnight when the original order didn't arrive in time for the customers wedding happening the next day. During my visit, a team member shared that once a client called looking for a discontinued pair of shoes. Zappos! didn't carry the style the client wanted so the Zappos! team member located it on another company's website and facilitated getting it for the customer. The Zappos! team members are encouraged to put the customer's needs at the center of everything they do on a daily basis which is the foundation of their reputation for having legendary customer service customers can depend on. [4]

Why do we trust them – Reason #3
Human approach to layoffs

Zappos! laid off 8% of their staff in 2008.Tony Hsieh stuck to his core values of transparency. There was no PR spin using fancy business speak about transformation, re-engineering or "right-sizing." Instead, Hsieh wrote an email to employees on Nov 6, 2008, the day of the layoffs, which was also posted on their public blog, sharing that the need for the cuts was to support the long-term financial health of the organization. The email is laced with humility. Hsieh provided extensive information on the financial position of the organization and why they needed to take this action. They also committed to providing a generous severance package which significantly exceeds what is required by law, including reimbursing laid off employees for a portion of their contribution for health benefits for that year. He acknowledged the family environment they've created together and how that makes it even more emotional for everyone at the company. The email was straight-forward, transparent and exhibited humility as the CEO educated the employees on the organization's financial situation and why this action was taken at this time.

There was a follow up email on Nov 11 after the weekend to those employees who remained, providing encouragement that together they will build an even stronger organization. He stated that the company didn't belong to him or the shareholders but rather belonged to everyone, including the employees.[5]

Why do we trust them – Reason #4 (I squeezed in an extra reason)

Zappos! produces a Culture Book each year

Each year, Zappos! staff produce a Culture Book that documents employee activity throughout the year. This book is used to document, highlight and celebrate the culture at Zappos!. Ironically, customers (like me) have ordered copies of the culture book online. The Culture Book is like a fancy yearbook that features employees living the Zappos! values.

Chapter 5: High Trust Company Profile - Zappos!

Zappos! wants to be an example and inspiration to other organizations to focus on having engaged, happy employees as a core principle that drives the innovation and passion to deliver superior business results.

Chapter 6:
It's Just Business?

As I mentioned earlier, I had to lay off six people from my team on the eventful Tuesday. I had a pretty close relationship with my overall team and I had hired some of the individuals I terminated that day. I knew who had just purchased a home. I knew whose partner took a leave from their job to go back to school. I knew the names and ages of their children. I inherently believe it's important to get to know my team however this knowledge isn't helpful on the morning when you're preparing to lay them off.

I believe it's my job as a people leader to execute the organization's strategy through my team. Organizational issues come up and decisions need to be made. In some cases, my input will be solicited and I can relay my perspective on the best course of action. Sometimes, my input will not be requested. Sometimes, I'll agree with the organization's decision and sometimes I won't. Regardless, it's my job to execute the decision and progress on the path forward. If I find myself in a scenario where I disagree with the organization more often than I agree, I should probably assess if the organization is a good fit for me.

This "communication spin" about the round of layoffs which I describe in the chapter ***Losing my corporate innocence***,

Chapter 6: It's Just Business?

marked the first major disconnect I had with the organization's approach. The managers receive a great deal of support and guidance from the human resources teams on how to handle the termination discussions. I decided that the best I could do was treat each person with respect and empathy. This conversation is often blindsiding in the moment and people may not even fully process what's happening until much later.

An example of this is George Clooney's role as Ryan Bingham in the 2009 film "Up In The Air." Ryan is a corporate downsizer who flies around the country to lay people off for corporate leaders who would rather not face their team members and have the difficult conversation. It's easier to outsource this task to a stranger contracted from another company. In the movie, Clooney plays Ryan, who is charged with training new employee Natalie Keener, played by Anna Kendrick. Throughout the movie Ryan and Natalie handle the emotional break down of employees just learning they have been laid off after, in some cases, decades of service. They manage the situation in a matter-of-fact manner with scripted speaking notes. They offer trite statements like:

"I know this is difficult for you."
"Some people find their true passion after being laid off."
"This may actually be a great new beginning for you."
"There is lots of support for you outlined in this package to help you start this new chapter in your life".

After shadowing Ryan for a few weeks, Natalie offers what she believes to be a brilliant and cost saving idea. Instead of travelling around the country and meeting with employees in person, why not set up a system that allowed them to fire people remotely. The employee logs into a computer with their corporate email address and a passcode that is provided prior to the meeting. Then, Ryan, Natalie or one of their colleagues runs through the carefully prepared script to let the employee know that unfortunately their services are no longer needed by the organization. Nothing says we value our employees more than hiring an outsourcing company and having complete strangers layoff long-tenured employees on a Zoom call.

In the movie, the remote initiative is quickly shelved after a video layoff goes horribly wrong.

So, on that fateful Tuesday in October, I got through the six layoff discussions. I did my best. That evening I emailed a fellow manager who also had a sizable number of layoffs to complete. I asked him how he was doing. He quickly emailed me back that he was fine. He let me know that as far as he was concerned, "….it's just business".

Is it just business?

If you want to manage people, you'll have to fire someone at some point. I wasn't overcome with sadness that October afternoon as I prepared to layoff my team members. I was doing my job. I didn't organize a telethon to create a college fund for their children. I have witnessed first-hand how these unexpected changes, usually unwanted, can truly land us in a better situation when we get to the other side of it. I'm tactful enough to know that I need to be careful when I share this truth. As a human being who has been disappointed many times, I am aware that this is the very last thing we want to hear when we are in the initial stages of processing a big, unwelcome change.

I was, however, saddened by the temporary stress the layoffs would have created for these six individuals and their families as they would naturally worry about the future. Everyone survived and as predicted, some went on to better opportunities.

Chapter 6: It's Just Business?

I thought that my moment of empathy and sadness after laying off my team members compared to my colleague's response was yet another piece of evidence that I wasn't corporate material. The list of evidence was getting pretty long.

I have since learned that there was absolutely nothing wrong with my response. This was my way of dealing with it. Perhaps the perceived callousness of my colleague was just a coping mechanism for him.

I'm surprised by how easily many of us can shrug off the callous actions of a corporation as "it's just business." "It's a big, profit-driven business." "Don't be naïve, Dionne. They don't care about you beyond the next dollar you can make or save for them."

Generating a healthy profit is the responsibility of any strong for-profit organization to ensure they are around for the long term for its employees, customers, and the communities it serves. Building trusting relationships with customers and employees is how organizations can play a large role to ensure their long-term success. At times, profit maximization will be in conflict with an organization's values at which time, values should win.

Why do we accept the assumption that being profit-driven and caring about people are conflicting concepts? Why is it so difficult to believe that high trust organizations generate better financials results?

"It's just business" is a cop out

I see it this way: every day, we hold hands and rejoice in concepts like trust and living our core values. Then, one day, the organization veers away from its stated principles.

Perhaps they change the compensation plan of commission-based sales people mid-year as more salespeople than anticipated are tracking to over-achieve and generate large commission payouts.

Maybe they remove a popular employee perk, like half-day Fridays during the summer months, without any communication about why this action is needed beyond a generic statement about increasing productivity and cutting costs.

Perhaps after a long tradition of promoting from within the company, a number of strategic roles are filled with external hires with no commentary from the leadership team.

At this point you can rely on someone shrugging their shoulders and saying "it's just business." It's like a get-out-of-jail free card for the leadership team. It's like saying, sure we'll be principled when it's easy to do so, but when things get tough, all bets are off. But don't worry, once things settle back down, we'll go back to focusing on building trust.

Trust deepens when we make hard decisions to stick to our principles

We are not considered to be principled until we demonstrate that we will stick to our values even in the most difficult moments.

Being high trust doesn't mean that it's tulips and honey every day. Strong leaders make difficult and unpopular decisions when needed because it's in the best long-term interest of the organization. In these moments, we demonstrate to our employees that we value them by engaging them and letting them understand why the change was necessary. Sincerely listen to their input and concerns. Always treat people with respect.

Chapter 6: It's Just Business?

I feel compelled to comment on the practice of adjusting salespeople's commissions mid-year. I've observed this being done a couple of times and the fallout was always deeply damaging. This may not be a contract breach as most organizations have clauses that would accommodate this type of change. It is, however, a breach of trust with your salesforce. The reality may be that there were some miscalculations in the original sales plan and some unexpectedly favourable conditions in the marketplace however the perception will be that you are penalizing your salesteam for doing the very thing you need them to do which is perform. If a change needs to be made to the sales commission structure, it should absolutely be made, in time for the beginning of the next sales year. Would the organization change the commission structure in circumstances where salespeople's results are lower than expected? Moving the finish line or adding in new activities mid-year which will make it more difficult for salespeople to achieve their sales results is simply unfair. It's the equivalent of starting to play a board game then changing the rules on everyone when it appears that you're going to lose.

This type of change illuminates the powerlessness some employees feel within large organizations. An action like changing the sales commission plan mid-year to reduce the overall compensation of salespeople feels like the big organization showing the employee who the boss is and who has the power. Although technically, that is the power differential, healthy, positive work cultures operate like it's a reciprocal relationship between the company and the employee. You'll come and work with us and we'll pay you what we agreed in your employment contract. While you're here, we'll give you a great work environment to learn and grow and you'll do your best work so we can grow this business together. High trust organizations operate under this guiding principle of reciprocal value being exchanged between the organization and its employees.

Suppose clients perceive their relationship with us as "just business?"

I've worked in a marketing role and can attest to the effort and expense organizations go to in order to convince clients that it's NOT just business and we are so much more than just a product or service. We have knowledgeable staff. We truly care about you and helping you to live your best life.

If you're like me you may have been moved to tears by commercials that pull at our heart strings about how our technology will help grandparents connect to their grandchildren miles away over the holidays. How our products and services will help you to save enough to go on that dream vacation or finance your aspiration of starting a business. Our anti-lock brakes and 4-wheel drive will keep your family safe for long drives. It's not just business. We want a personal relationship with you. We want you to see us as an invaluable partner in your life.

If our customers thought their engagement with us was "just business" that would be problematic for most companies. It means we are transactional to our customers and easily replaceable by another company or even an online tool. When it's "just business":

- Clients don't have a compelling reason why they are doing business specifically with us and can easily get the same products and services from a competitor. There's nothing driving loyalty.
- Clients would always choose the lowest price offer

Chapter 6: It's Just Business?

- Clients would leave us for the slightest issue or inconvenience

"Its just business" is a losing strategy

My point here is that "its just business" is a losing strategy found in low trust organizations. It fosters a transactional relationship with our employees as well as our customers. I'm sure you, like me, have observed team members whose philosophy turns to "I'm just here to do my job and go home". They give nothing less and nothing more than what is required of them. This is a depressing environment to work in where it's clear people are at work under the duress of having to earn a living to pay their bills. Imagine how inspiring it is for your customers to engage with your employees who reluctantly work for your organization. It results in employees who blindly follow rules and don't feel compelled to go over and above or to accommodate customers where possible.

This happens when there's distrust between the leadership team and their employees. Every action or new initiative announced by leadership is met with predictable skepticism as employees try to figure out what the ulterior motive is. Even a seemingly positive initiative to revamp the employee benefits plan is met with the suspicion that somehow employees are getting screwed in the process and probably getting less value and paying more.

The extra time needed to overcome this skepticism with employees and try to gain buy-in for every new change can be exhausting for middle managers. Trying to unlock creative problem solving and ideas for continuous improvement in this type of environment can feel impossible.

"Its just business" is a losing strategy. Being committed to corporate values and fostering trust is how high trust organizations operate all the time, its not a strategy that's followed intermittently when its convenient to do so.

Chapter 7:
High Trust Company Profile Berkshire Hathaway

I watched a biography on Warren Buffett, CEO of Berkshire Hathaway. The concept of trust permeated the entire documentary and I knew I had to include his company in my profiles on trust. I'm used to reading about inspired companies that grow to the point of being taken over by investment holding companies like Berkshire Hathaway. The next step is typically for these holding companies to extract maximum value from the underlying organization pressuring the leadership teams of the underlying companies to squeeze cost at every turn to improve returns to investors. Being fiscally responsible is always a good thing but it's common for cost cutting to be made at the expense of some of the defining components of a company's core value to its stakeholders. Premium ingredients may be replaced with less expensive alternatives. Employee perks that drive high loyalty rates may be watered down to standard industry practices.

Berkshire Hathaway is about creating value over time and trusting leadership teams to do the right thing. Berkshire

Hathaway hires primarily for integrity which is key. Jim Weber, an executive at BH states, "I have never been given so much autonomy in my long business career, and have never felt so accountable and responsible."[1]

What does Berkshire Hathaway do?

Berkshire Hathaway is a holding company that owns a multitude of companies and sells shares to its investors to raise capital and share profits. Berkshire Hathaway stocks are currently the most expensive publicly traded stock.

What is their position within the industry?

BH ranked number 6 in Forbes Fortune 500 company listing.[2]

Why do we trust them – Reason #1

Reciprocal trust between CEOs and Buffett

Berkshire Hathaway invests in good companies with strong leadership that don't need micromanagement. The CEOs of these companies under the Berkshire Hathaway umbrella are given a level of autonomy unprecedented in other similar organizations to run their businesses. They submit their financials on a regular basis and speak with Warren when needed. They are trusted to run their companies.

There's reciprocity of trust between the CEOs and Buffett.[3]

Why do we trust them – Reason #2

When they fumble, they course correct and ultimately do the right thing

David Sokol was a trusted team member in Berkshire Hathaway and Buffett tasked him with finding new acquisition opportunities. Sokol became interested in a company named

Chapter 7: High Trust Company Profile Berkshire Hathaway

Lubrizol with the intent to pitch the company to Buffett. The issue is that Sokol first purchased $10 million in Lubrizol shares. When Berkshire Hathaway ultimately purchased the company, it was a direct financial benefit for Sokol. When this became known, Sokol agreed to resign amidst the conflict of interest scandal. Buffett's initial statement about Sokol's resignation was not as strong as investors would have liked and seemed to play down the controversy. Buffett subsequently requested an independent audit whose results had much stronger language than Buffett's initial statement. The audit concluded that Sokol had violated Berkshire Hathaway policy and put the company's reputation at risk. Buffett followed up with a stronger statement following the audit denouncing Sokol's actions.[4]

Why do we trust them – Reason #3
Hire trustworthy people then trust them

Berkshire Hathaway hires primarily for integrity. They hire trustworthy people then trust them deeply which inspires a sense pride and accountability that supports the organization's culture. They have over 300,000 employees yet they have had very few scandals. They don't have the large compliance departments found in many large organizations. Ironically, most of the organizations involved in the 2008 financial crisis had some of the largest compliance departments. You can't monitor people into compliance and ethical behaviour. Hire people with high integrity and the issue of ethics diminishes.[5]

Chapter 8:
Do Organizations need to be high trust to be successful?

In a perfect world, the answer would be a resounding YES! Alas, trustworthiness is optional when it comes to an organization's financial performance. You don't need to look far to find a large public company whose track record in fostering trust is pretty sparse but produces strong quarterly and annual performance for its investors.

I have a monthly service with a large corporation. The deal is that I give them a substantial amount of money each month and they provide me with internet and phone service as well as network cable stations that I rarely watch. I've been their client for decades. When everything is running smoothly, things are good primarily because we don't speak to each other. They don't call me and I don't call them. We don't speak. We have a functionally dysfunctional relationship.

But on those occasions when something goes wrong or I need to make a change to a component of my service, I pre-emptively take two Advil, drink a cup of chamomile tea, and read my book

Chapter 8: Do Organizations need to be high trust to be successful?

of positive affirmations before calling their customer service number. I have very low trust that they care about my level of satisfaction with their products and services. This opinion isn't just me being cynical. I assure you the organization earned my low opinion of them through years of neglecting my needs as a customer often making me feel like they were doing me a favour by allowing me to be their client. On a positive note, they are responsible for me choosing to start a regular meditation practice immediately following one of my calls with one of their customer service team members.

Some history

I recognize I share some of the responsibility for my rocky relationship with this company. You see, I made things profoundly complicated for the company by moving into my new home a couple of weeks before leaving my old residence. I always overlap time when I move to make things easier for myself. The issue is that the company's systems can't manage this scenario. According to their operating system, everyone leaves a residence and moves into the new residence on the same calendar day. This means that rather than seamlessly transferring my services to the new residence on the same day, they would have to open a brand-new account for me at my new residence and then cancel the old one once I move out. I would therefore have two accounts with them for a couple of weeks.

The cancelling of one account and creating a new account results in two issues for me:
1. My email account invariably gets cancelled in the process which is one of the easiest ways to throw my world into chaos.

2. It triggers a hefty cancellation fee which is not charged if you continue service with them.

I discovered my email was cancelled when I started to get text messages from friends and business associates letting me know my emails were bouncing back. I contacted their call centre, trying to remain calm as my call was being recorded for training purposes. My call was answered by an incredibly pleasant and polite customer service representative who patiently explained to me that my email was attached to the old account, not the new account, so when I cancelled my old account, it would naturally be cancelled. She highlighted to me it would have been easily addressed if I had told them not to cancel the email service on the old account. I calmly explained that when I said "include all the same services I currently have" in my new account, I was being literal. I didn't know I had to explicitly note that I need my email service too. I would have needed to have their procedure manual on hand to have been able to communicate to them more accurately in a manner they required.

In lieu of the expletives that were on the tip of my tongue, I asked sarcastically if there was a procedural manual that they published for clients that I may be able to study for future calls. She politely said there was no such manual. She then asked me if she had addressed all my needs and requested that I complete a short survey on my experience with them that day.

After having that issue resolved, about a month later I received a bill for my old account with an outstanding amount owing. By now I had started my meditation practice so after a few minutes of centering myself while listening to my audio of waves crashing on the beach, I called their customer service number and inquired about the cost. Another polite and pleasant customer

Chapter 8: Do Organizations need to be high trust to be successful?

service representative diligently looked into it then explained it's my cancellation fee. The system didn't recognize that I was continuing my service with a new account and assumed I was discontinuing service with them. The cancellation triggered a fee which he proceeded to reverse for me which I thought was very decent of him since the fee was the result of their system limitation.

    I know, issues happen. I agree that we need to be patient. I would add that with large corporations, upgrades to core technology systems can be prohibitively expensive particularly when they have acquired smaller organizations over the years and have a number of operating systems working together. Fixing all of the issues will deplete the organization of the funds it needs to grow its business. I'm not a simpleton. I know that it's often better to work around these issues than to fix them.

    I also recognize with large corporations you can't control the experience a client has with every single customer service agent. There could be hundreds of agents depending on the size of the organization. Some are within the organization and some may be working for a third-party company working on behalf of the main organization. When an issue is identified, it can take months and sometimes years to address those service issues through training or even replacing some individuals on the team.

    I could conclude that this was just a bad experience I had with a well-meaning organization at a time when they were challenged by some aspects of their customer service that they expediently addressed.

    I moved three times over the next five years, and, sadly, I encountered the exact same issues I outlined above each and every time. Selfishly, I keep overlapping my moves to make my own life easier. After my first move, I became a more savvy customer and would emphasize to the person processing my move request, "make sure you don't cancel my email service" and "ensure you don't charge me the cancellation fee." I created my own client procedural manual I use each time I call them. Each time, they assure me they captured my request in the notes and each time, my email service got cancelled and I was always charged a cancellation fee.

It turns out the organization had a very effective workaround for their system issues. I was the workaround. You see, when I started to get text messages from my contacts advising me that my emails were getting bounced back, that was the trigger for me to call and alert them to the problem and have them reinstate my email service. To their credit, they always rectified the problem once I called.

Then, like clockwork, I would receive a final bill with a cancellation fee which would trigger me to call them, explain to them exactly what happened as I am now an expert, and ask them to fix it for me. Sometimes I'm angry when I call. Sometimes I'm frustrated. Sometimes I'm indifferent. It depends on my mood.

I know, it could just be three random occasions of bad luck on my part. Maybe I'm just being a bit dramatic, but then something else happened.

I went to see one of my favourite comedians at a venue that holds about 2,700 people. As part of his act, the comedian relayed an experience with the same company which he named. The details were different but the bottom line was that their customer service is horrendous. A venue full of people howled. It was clear that we were not howling because of his comedic retelling of an isolated, unfortunate experience. We were all laughing with him because it was a fairly universal experience

Chapter 8: Do Organizations need to be high trust to be successful?

including the frustrating call ending with the representative cheerfully asking us if they were able to address all of our concerns and asking us to complete a short, automated survey as smoke billows out of our ears. It was hilarious because it resonated so deeply with the crowd and we took solace in the shared experience.

I remember thinking to myself that I would be aghast if I was a leader in an organization that was being roasted so publicly.

It doesn't have to be this way. Let's consider that at one end of the spectrum, we have the option to spend a boat-load of money on slick technology to permanently fix these issues and at the other end of the spectrum, you piss off the customer who phones, infuriated, to your customer service line complaining about the service. I suggest that between these two extremes, there are a multitude of more cost-efficient and client-friendly solutions.

The conclusion I have drawn, rightly or wrongly, is that this organization just doesn't care enough to improve my experience. Their main competitor has a similar reputation so I don't really have anywhere to go. Both companies have strong financial results and are widely celebrated successful organizations. Their annual reports are littered with content about how highly they value and appreciate their clients. I continue to tolerate their service. Currently there aren't any viable alternatives for me, but when one shows up, I will be the first one out the door despite my decades of forced loyalty to this company.

That's my long-winded and animated way of say, no, fostering high trust is not a pre-requisite of being a financially successful organization. In **Part 3: Show me the money**, I'll explain the "low trust tax" this company is paying and the financial benefits they are foregoing by not holding trust as one of their core values.

It comes down to the values of the organization and its leaders. It's about the reputation you want to have as an organization. It's about the impact you want to have on your employees, clients and the communities you serve.

It's about whether or not you would lose sleep knowing that an auditorium of 2,700 people were laughing heartily at your appalling customer service.

Chapter 9:
High Trust Company Profile - Method

I was first introduced to the Method brand of environmentally-friendly cleaning products when I attended the "The Art of Marketing" conference in Toronto almost ten years ago. Method's co-founder, Eric Ryan did the presentation under the pseudonym "Method Man." He was inspiring, insightful and irreverent. Founders Eric Ryan and Adam Lowry are so proudly weird. Ever since that day, you can always find Method products all over my home. Sure, they have great design and scents, but they are also effective and environmentally friendly.

I've since researched the company, including reading their book **The Method Method** and somehow I like them even more. Their weirdness permeates everything they do and inspires their creativity and unconventional approach.

I have to share one of my most favourite stories about them that they share in their book. They regularly used an image of a daisy in their ads as a visual representation of gentleness and nature. It turns out that Clorox had also used a daisy in some of their ads and sent a strongly worded letter from their lawyers demanding that Method cease and desist from ever using the daisy again. If you're Method, there's only one appropriate response to this situation. They created a website, posted the cease and desist Clorox letter on the site and urged the public to vote on who should own the daisy, Clorox, Method, or Mother Earth. How brilliant. Mother Earth won by a landslide, and Method never heard from Clorox again on the matter of the daisy. They made a very loud point which resonated with their supporters. Their book is filled with authentic, meaningful and fun ways to connect with your like-minded community. I am a lifelong fan of Method.

What does Method do?

Method manufactures cleaning products. They specialize in effective, environmentally friendly products that have great design.

What is their position within the industry?

Method has sales in excess of $100 million annually.[1]

Why do we trust them – Reason #1

Focus on culture as a competitive advantage.

In their book ***The Method Method***, Eric Ryan and Adam Lowry, the founders of Method share that they wanted to create a culture that would "inspire and enable us to do our best work while fostering a workplace that enriches our lives."[2] They note that many leaders underestimate the power of culture especially when resources are tight. They recall the typical response would be to focus on the business metrics first then look at culture as an after-thought. I love the analogy they use in the book. They describe this way of thinking as the equivalent of a coach of a sports team saying, "once we start winning, we'll get everyone

Chapter 9: High Trust Company Profile - Method

motivated and playing as a team." The founders saw culture as their competitive advantage that leads to great talent leaving prestigious jobs at other, more established, companies to join them and putting in long hours.

As Method grew, they were intentional about maintaining a great culture and rejected the process and procedure they perceived a human resources department or other traditional forms of organization would introduce. Method formed a Value Pod which included a group of employees representing all departments and created their values which they refer to as the Methodology:

- Keep Method weird
- What would MacGyver do?
- Innovate, don't imitate
- Collaborate, collaborate, collaborate
- Care like crazy

I'll just touch on the one that's probably the least intuitive. "What would MaGyver do?" MacGyver was a popular TV series in the 1980's. Angus MacGyver is a brilliantly resourceful undercover government agent who would outsmart the bad guys in each weekly episode. The extent of his resourcefulness borders on the ridiculous. Method considers MacGyver to be a company mascot and they channel his resourceful approach into everything they do. I think creating a mascot for the organization is ingenious. I must admit that when I find myself in a challenging situation with no clear solution, I find myself whispering to myself, "what would MacGyver do?"

Why do we trust them – Reason #2
They seek to find advocates and some become customers

Method is helping to lead the movement to more environmentally friendly, healthy cleaning products. Rather than pushing products, they educate people about what's in their products and encourage them to be more informed consumers. All of this is delivered in a fun, quirky manner that's more lighthearted than any of their competitors. By default, they are also highlighting the benefits of their products and hope that their innovative products and designs will convert some of those advocates into customers. So far it's working with their target market, who care deeply about the environment, healthy living in the home and appreciate great design. They align with their customers on values.

Why do we trust them – Reason #3
Providing job opportunities with their new manufacturing plant "the Soapbox"

Method built a sustainable factory in Pullman, an underserved community located on the south side of Chicago. They chose this location for very practical reasons based on its proximity to railways which have a smaller carbon footprint than trucks. They are right on the Great Lakes. Additionally, they wanted to bring new jobs and training to the Pullman community which has suffered since many manufacturing plants moved out of the area over the past few decades. Method fulfilled its commitment to hire locally wherever possible with the intent to train people lacking manufacturing experience. They launched a campaign called "There's Beauty Inside" which has multiple connotations. They are referring to the beauty in the

Chapter 9: High Trust Company Profile - Method

content of their products. The beauty of the design of their containers. The beauty in the people who work in the Soapbox who make the difference in their products.

Of the 22 acres that belong to the plant, only 4 acres are used for the factory facility and the rest of the property is being restored to be a home for Illinois' indigenous people. A third of the energy needed to run the facility is generated through wind and solar energy. There's a greenhouse on the roof which provides 50 tons of produce distributed throughout the Chicago area.

Chapter 10:
What About Creating Shareholder Value?

In 1970, the economist Milton Friedman wrote the article, "The social responsibility of a business is to increase its profits." This laid the foundation for the philosophy that dominated business from the 1980s into the first decade of the new millennium, that the primary purpose of a business is to build the wealth of its shareholders.[1] Finally, in 2019, The Business Roundtable, a community of almost 200 CEOs of major US corporations, issued a statement changing the purpose of a corporation to focus on creating value for all of its stakeholders including customers, investing in employees and ethically dealing with suppliers and outside communities.

I landed in the corporate world during its love affair with its shareholders and obsession with creating value for them was the priority. It was drilled into our heads as employees. It felt like it was our purpose for getting out of bed in the morning. We had to cut costs to provide shareholder value. We needed to downsize to remain competitive and create shareholder value. We needed to print double-sided and use recycled paper to create shareholder value.

Chapter 10: What About Creating Shareholder Value?

It felt like our operating budget belonged to shareholders. It did not belong to us and above all else, we needed to keep that dominant in our mind and behave accordingly. The ongoing success of the organization was predicated on the organization's ability to maintain its current capital and attract more through providing strong shareholder value by constantly increasing share value.

It felt like these nameless, faceless shareholders were omnipresent in my daily professional life.

Why did I reject the concept of shareholder primacy?

I wholeheartedly rejected the concept of shareholder primacy from the first time it was relayed to me. I didn't reject the concept because I felt these shareholders where metaphorically looking over my shoulder each day to ensure my actions would extract the highest value for them. Was that annoying? Yes. But that wasn't the cause of my discontent

I didn't reject it because I had researched and developed an alternative and compelling philosophy that provided stronger corporate performance.

I rejected the concept of the primacy of creating shareholder value because it simply never made any sense to me. In fact, it was probably one of the craziest concepts I had ever heard in a business context.

My reasoning was very simple, how the fuck could the purpose of an organization be to maximize shareholder profit?

Did Walt Disney open Disneyland in July of 1955 with a rigorous focus of creating shareholder value?

Did Steve Jobs invent the iPod with the sole purpose of creating shareholder value?

I know Yvon Chouinard never had shareholder value on his mind in 1973 when he started making clothing for rock climbers in the early days of his company Patagonia.

Selling their product and making a profit was surely a motivation. Any responsible company strives to operate at a profit. If they aren't fiscally prudent, then they jeopardize the long-term viability of the company. Customers would lose access to their product or service and employees would lose their jobs.

These companies sought to deliver a strong customer value proposition. The proposition was very different for each of them but they were each focused on the customer and solving problems for their customer at a profit.

Disneyland wanted to be the "happiest place on earth". Steve Jobs wanted to put 1,000 songs in our pockets and Patagonia just wants us to get outside and embrace nature.

I can spring out of bed in the morning, excited about spending my day solving interesting problems. The thought of being a cog in the wheel of a large corporation with the sole purpose of generating strong returns for shareholders is a reason to snooze my alarm at least 8 times before I reluctantly drag myself out of bed while contemplating if I should call in sick and go back to bed.

If you're thinking, isn't creating shareholder value synonymous with building a profitable, sustainable business? Absolutely not. There are overlaps but they aren't the same. In practice, the term "creating shareholder value" has evolved over the years to mean that a company operates at a profit and those profits are delivered consistently in 3 month increments each year. The stock price should increase consistently quarter-over-quarter and year-over-year. Any drop is seen as

Chapter 10: What About Creating Shareholder Value?

a stumble that the leadership team needs to expediently rectify to get their share price back on its upward trajectory.

CEOs would join phone calls with analysts, industry journalists, managers of mutual funds, pension plans, hedge funds and others each quarter. How is the business doing? What's the strategic plan? How are you tracking to that plan? Do you foresee any challenges? How will you address those challenges? Are there any upcoming big decisions? Are you going to hit your financial projections?

This information would be packaged and published across the industry to investors. The premise is that increasing share value is the primary goal. Up is always good.

I found the whole cycle a little confusing yet, this appeared to be the universally accepted process. What was wrong with me? I have never considered myself to be the smartest person in the room and accordingly, I accepted that I just didn't get this corporate world. At the time, I didn't have an MBA and I definitely didn't have any specialized education in financial markets. I was only a few years out of university and quite junior in my career. I decided that all of this share analysis and shareholder obsession must be over my head so best that I keep my thoughts to myself lest I expose myself as a neophyte.

What about customers?

Instead of this obsession with shareholders, what about being obsessed with customers? One of my all-time favourite business thought leaders is Peter Drucker. Drucker's management philosophies have been described as the foundation for modern management. So much of his writing resonates with me and I love what he defines as the purpose of business. According to Drucker, "the purpose of business is to create and keep a customer."[2] That's an idea I would get out of bed for. How can we increase value and wow our customers?

Of course, there was a discussion about customers and new products and promotions but at any town hall, the shareholder value story was always the headline.

I'm so pleased and reassured to see modern business management culture has shifted away from the servitude to the shareholder towards creating value for customers, employees, suppliers and our communities, as documented by the 2019 Business Round Table.[3] Jack Welch, the iconic leader of GE through the 1980s and 1990s was the mascot for shareholder primacy as demonstrated by his management philosophy. In 2009, after his retirement and with the hindsight of the 2008 financial crisis, Welch famously described the primacy of shareholder value as "the dumbest idea in the world. Shareholder value is a result, not a strategy... your main constituencies are your employees, your customers and your products."[4]

Hmmm. Maybe I was onto something.

These tides have been changing for a while. Lynn Stout is a professor of Corporate and Business Law at Cornell Law School whose work has been cited by US Supreme Court justices. Lynn is also the brilliant author of the book *The Shareholder Value Myth*. In her book, she lays out a comprehensive argument that heralding the creation of shareholder value as the primary goal of business hurts just about every stakeholder: customers, employees, communities and some shareholders.

Shareholders are not a homogenous group

A foundational argument in Stout's book is that pursuing the creation of shareholder value assumes that shareholders are a homogeneous group of individuals with aligned goals. This is

Chapter 10: What About Creating Shareholder Value?

untrue. There are long-term investors looking for capital gains over the long term. There are shareholders who actively trade, the most active of whom are day traders. There are shareholders who invest for the purpose of regular dividend payments. When we become obsessed with the quarterly results, we are actually only focusing on the best interest of short-term investors who are looking for a quick cash gain over a few hours, days, weeks or months. Shareholders are not a homogeneous group with identical goals so pursuing shareholder value is problematic.

It's like a radio station saying it wants to attract music lovers. Well, which ones? There are music lovers who love hip hop, classical, country, gospel, top 40, soca, blue grass, rock, reggaeton, EDM, opera, rap, show tune musical scores, dancehall, heavy metal, afrobeats, etc. Then we have music lovers who enjoy more than one genre. There is no single strategy to generically attract music lovers just like there isn't a single strategy to satisfy all shareholders.

In order to build and maintain a profitable organization over the long term there are periods of time when the company may need to take a short term hit in returns in order to invest in initiatives and strategies that are meant to set the organization up for long-term success. There can be foundational initiatives that puts critical functionality or capability in place to propel the long-term business strategy, make operations more efficient and fuel greater value creation for customers.

An organization that chooses to be beholden to its shareholders may forego some of these investments afraid of the short-term impact on their share price and financial results. This would be great for short-term investors but has been shown to be harmful for the long-term viability of the organization and its longer term investors. The goals of long-term investors are more closely aligned with the goals of the organization, its employees and its clients.

I don't want to give short term investors a bad name. Many of them are wonderful people who eat three servings of fruits and vegetables each day and shovel the driveway of elderly neighbours during the winter. Day trading is a great strategy for those who want to actively manage their investment portfolio. The issue only arises when our business leaders choose to align their leadership decisions and strategy to satisfy these short term investors. It's not helpful when the compensation plans for leaders in many of those organizations incent the leaders to this short-term thinking. Often, increases in share price rewards leaders with sizable cash bonuses and capital gains. Being a slave to shareholders can be financially lucrative for a leadership team.

The Shareholder myth

In Stout's book, she references the "shareholder myth". This myth was upheld based on the "efficient market hypothesis" which states that if a manager took a short-term action that would ultimately harm the long-term performance of the business, the marketplace would be aware there are longer term implications to the short-term bump in financial results. This awareness of the long-term implications would theoretically be factored into the value of the share eliminating any benefit in taking a short-term tactic to increase share value that would deliver longer term negative impacts. The "efficient market hypothesis" has been waning in popularity since the late 1980's when there have been numerous exceptions to this alleged rule. When your theory has an excessive number of exceptions, it ceases to be a credible theory.

Chapter 10: What About Creating Shareholder Value?

Consider that in 1960, only 12% of shares on the New York Stock Exchange turned over annually. Eighty years ago, buying and selling shares was onerous, costly and reserved to a small percentage of the public who owned and traded shares in public companies. You would call a stock broker and pay fees for buying and selling. Information for an individual investor to research their own stocks wasn't easily available and definitely not at the disposal of the average person. In his early investing days, Warren Buffett used to personally visit companies he planned to invest in so he could meet the management team and ask them details about their strategy, operations and performance. These details are readily available today to anyone with a decent wifi connection.

The number of investors has exploded and the cost of trading stocks is minimal with some accounts offering unlimited trades for a flat monthly fee. I can buy or sell a stock on my phone in the same time it takes me to order an Uber.

In the year 2000, considering all stock exchanges in the US, there was a 300% turnover rate. That means a large number of shareholders are transient. Why would a leadership team cater to these short-term investors? The tail doesn't wag the dog.

The way the system was meant to work is that companies go off and build great businesses with great employees. They create great products and services that win them customer loyalty and allow them to grow over time. Investors decide to invest in those companies that meet their investment goals. Everyone can happily co-exist.

Chapter 11:
High Trust Company Profile - Netflix

Netflix rescued me from a life of drowning in DVD late fees. I always meant to return the DVDs on time but it just never worked out that way. I wasn't an early fan of Netflix. I didn't subscribe to their DVD subscription service. My interest grew after their streaming service was featured as one of "Oprah's favourite things." When I finally started my Netflix subscription, a whole new world of online content opened up for me. In the early days, it was a small fraction of the content available today, but even then, it was huge. I learned how to binge watch with series like 24 but I elevated my binge watching skills to an artform with series on Netflix like Scandal and Arrested Development.

Netflix has transformed how we watch television. I grew up in the era of three American television networks, ABC, NBC and CBS who would compete with each other for ratings. To be honest, if it weren't for my unhealthy obsession with HGTV and home renovation shows, I don't think I would even have cable.

Today Netflix has won 12 Academy Awards® for its original content. As people were locked down around the world

Chapter 11: High Trust Company Profile - Netflix

due to the COVID-19 pandemic, Netflix felt like an essential service by providing seemingly endless content to help keep us entertained. *The Crown* and *Bridgerton* were the perfect opportunity to distract us from the stream of bad news about the pandemic, the economy and other depressing topics being featured on television news stations.

What does Netflix do?

Netflix is a streaming service that offers a wide variety of commercial-free TV shows, movies, anime, and documentaries to subscribers who access the service online for a monthly subscription fee.

What is their position within the industry?

Netflix has over 50% of the market share in online streaming content with more than seven providers dividing up the remaining 50%.[1]

Why do we trust them – Reason #1

Created an iconic PowerPoint deck on building a strong culture

Reed Hastings, founder of Netflix, along with Patty McCord, the Chief Talent Officer for 14 years, pulled together a 127-page PowerPoint deck[2] that captured the effective leadership principles Netflix had championed since its inception. The deck has since gone viral. Netflix culture is described as Freedom & Responsibility. Consider that Netflix expense policy simply states to "act in Netflix's best interest."[3]

Why do we trust them – Reason #2
Vigilant to ensure they have motivated employees that can handle the freedom and responsibility

In 2002 Netflix laid off 30% of the 120 employees it had at the time due to economic pressures and surprisingly their business results took off. There were some marketplace developments that helped them but they found that some managers were happier with less employees. A manager shared that he wasted a lot of time managing his team members as well as checking and fixing their work. He was far more productive and happier with fewer team members to manage.

As their business evolved, they had to lay off some very strong employees whose skills no longer met the needs of the organization. Patty describes a scenario with a bookkeeper on their team who contributed significantly to the business' success however they now needed CPA's. They considered making up a role just to keep her, but decided that was the wrong thing to do and had an honest conversation with her, offered her a generous severance package and they amicably parted ways.

Netflix is committed to only maintain "A-players" on their team.[4]

Why do we trust them – Reason #3
Hire Mature Adults who can be relied on to exercise good judgement

Netflix rejects building a company bureaucracy with policies and extensive procedures as well as enforcing management oversight so managers are spending a significant amount of time just making sure people are doing what they're supposed to be doing. Netflix hires trustworthy, mature adults who can

Chapter 11: High Trust Company Profile - Netflix

be relied on to look out for the organization's best interests. Their experience, so far, is that this policy results in only a handful of instances where employees pursue an action that is at odds with what's best for the organization and can usually be resolved with a candid conversation. If there's a value disconnect, those individuals are expediently exited from the organization.

This is how Netflix was able to get rid of its vacation policy. It turns out that if they have a vacation policy, there are regulatory requirements to track and monitor time off. This tracking and monitoring went against the Netflix culture so they decided if they don't have a vacation policy, then there's no tracking or monitoring required. Instead, they tell employees to take time off as needed. There are principles that teams follow to ensure they have adequate staffing levels during busy periods so there's no disruption to business. You may think the result is that many employees don't take vacation at all. I know a number of corporations with extensive, detailed vacation policies that need to insist employees take their vacations. A busy team member may forego vacation to meet aggressive deliverables throughout the year. That's not the case at Netflix. The leadership model for their employees that they expect them to not just take time off but take long vacations to recharge. People regularly share details and pictures from their vacations with the executive team leading by example.[5]

Chapter 12:
Principles Over Profits

I recall attending a town hall once for a high trust company that prides itself in walking the talk. All manner of questions were posed by employees to the leadership team. One of the last questions in the Q&A uncovered an interesting and little-known pet peeve. A female employee complained that on the main floor at head office, there were more bathroom stalls in the men's washroom than the women's washroom, even though there were significantly more female employees at that location. She wondered how this made sense and wondered if it could be resolved, as it resulted in unnecessary lineups in the women's washroom.

Hmmm. The CEO thought for a minute then said, "no, that doesn't make any sense." Being a male, with his pick of bathroom stalls, he wasn't aware of the inconvenience endured by his female colleagues. Many females in the audience confirmed the validity of this inequity. He stated that as of the end of that town hall, women can use the men's washroom and vice versa on the main floor at head office. Upon returning to his office he wrote "Men" on a piece of 8x10 paper and "Women" on another sheet of paper and stuck it to the respective doors with scotch tape as the informal signal of the change. In the

Chapter 12: Principles Over Profits

meantime, property management was alerted to make the necessary construction changes to officially switch the washrooms.

That's being responsive.

In terms of raising and reinforcing the level of trust within your organization, the big wins are when the leadership team sticks to its core principles even when it's hard to do. The example above wasn't a valiant example of courage but rather, a simple demonstration that the leadership team is committed to removing issues that negatively impact employees, whether it's about faster decision making or eliminating line ups in the washroom.

In profit-seeking organizations, it can be difficult to pass up increased profits that would benefit the organization and its shareholders, some of whom are also employees. When you're leading from a place of integrity, your mission and vision are not just words on a poster or website but rather, employees can point to tangible actions the organization takes on a regular basis to live those values.

Let's take a look at some examples of companies and individuals who demonstrated tremendous courage to lead by their principles. They acted in alignment with their values with a strong certainty there would be short-term pain and no guarantee that it would pay off in the long-run. That's what true courage and acting with integrity looks like. That's what builds trust.

CVS decides that selling tobacco and promoting better health are incompatible[1]

October 1st, 2015 CVS Caremark, one of the largest pharmacy chains in the US decided to stop selling all tobacco products in its 7,600 US stores. Larry J. Merlo, the president and CEO of CVS Caremark at the time said that "put simply, the sale of tobacco products is inconsistent with our purpose" which is to "help people on their path to better health."

At the time the decision was made, CVS anticipated it would lose $1.5 billion in annual tobacco sales as well as an additional $500 thousand annually in additional goods that consumers would purchase while purchasing their tobacco products.

CVS lost $2 billion in revenue and upset many of its shareholders but it was just a short term hit and the company continues to thrive. Today CVS is championed for its fearless leadership.[2]

Unilever stopped providing quarterly financial updates[3]

By 2015, the average holding period for shares traded on the US stock exchanges was 17 weeks representing a 300% annual turnover rate. Compare that to 1960 when the average holding period for Unilever stocks was 12 years. Paul Polman, CEO for Unilever, was focused on building the organization for long-term growth and sustainability by investing in the fundamentals of the business. He grew increasingly concerned about the negative impact this short-term line of sight by investors had on his ability to lead and manage an organization for the long-term.[4]

In 2009, Polman courageously announced that he would stop providing quarterly financial updates and guidance. Immediately, Unilever stock dropped 8% and he lost many short-term investors. This was fine with Polson as his intention was to attract shareholders who were in alignment with Unilever's long-term strategy. Unilever would then invest in

Chapter 12: Principles Over Profits

capital ventures that would take longer to deliver returns but would position the business well for the future.

Polman never believed in the trade-off between short-term and long-term organizational success. He went on to state, "it is a cop-out. Any CEO can decide that he shouldn't get paid too much. Any CEO can decide to think long term... I think it is courageous leadership that is missing. The excuse is that the market won't let you... we have a license that is much broader than any of the CEOs claim."[5]

Paul Polman decided to be the change he wanted to see in the world.

Netflix & Dave Chapelle

It's a sad reality that many young artists find themselves in contracts that are overwhelmingly skewed in favour of the large organization and often give up their rights to their creative product. Being young, desperate to make it into the business and often financially constrained, many new artists see their first contract as the reward they have been working so hard towards and dreaming about. Some artists hesitate to push back too hard on any seemingly unfair clauses fearing the contract could be withdrawn without warning. Years later, older, wiser, more savvy and with more sophisticated legal representation, they realize just how skewed those initial agreements are in favour of the organization over the artist. This is exactly what happened to Dave Chapelle.

His wildly popular show *The Dave Chapelle Show* aired from 2003 to 2006 on Comedy Central. It turns out that in the contract Dave signed, Comedy Central had the right to license out the program without providing Dave with any compensation or notice. That's precisely what Comedy Central did selling the streaming rights to Netflix and HBO Max.

Dave decided to call up Netflix with whom he currently has a contract. His argument wasn't a legal one. Comedy Central acted within the terms of the contract. Chapelle argued instead that it "wasn't right" for his art to be streamed without his knowledge or compensation. Netflix agreed and decided to pull *The Dave Chapelle Show*.

Dave eloquently summed up Netflix culture in a manner that only Dave could deliver. "That's why I fuck with Netflix, because they pay me my money, they do what they say they're gonna do," Chappelle said in the video. "And they went above and beyond what you could expect from a businessman."[6]

American Airlines provides a mid-contract pay increase to pilots and flight attendants[7]

American Airlines had completed their contract negotiations with their pilots and flight attendants in early 2015. Throughout the rest of 2015, the other airlines renegotiated their staff contracts at a higher pay rate than what American Airlines had negotiated. Some may interpret that as lucky timing for American Airlines to lock in lower rates early in the game. Many financial analysts considered this to be a fortuitous win for American Airlines and were blindsided when American Airlines leadership didn't see it that way.

American Airlines was experiencing trust issues within its employee base and their CEO, Doug Parker, was concerned their early contract negotiations would be perceived mistakenly by staff as a strategic move by management to lock them into rates lower than the industry. In response, Parker, in an

Chapter 12: Principles Over Profits

act of goodwill, announced that they would increase base rates mid-contract to ensure their employees were being paid competitively.

The financial markets were not impressed. One JPMorgan analyst wrote, "We are troubled by AAL's wealth transfer of nearly $1 billion to its labor groups. In addition to raising fixed costs, American's agreement with its labor stakeholders establishes a worrying precedent, in our view, both for American and the industry."[8]

American's stock took a 9% hit which lasted two weeks until that value rebounded. By the end of the year, it was up 20%.[9]

Costco endures pressure to cut wages and benefits

Costco has a long history of providing one of the most attractive compensation packages in retail. They post strong financial returns each year but analysts wonder how much more they could be earning if they reduced their compensation package.

"I just think people need to make a living wage with health benefits," says Craig Jelinek, Costco CEO. "It also puts more money back into the economy and creates a healthier country. It's really that simple."[10] Those are Jelinek's principles and he's sticking to them.

Taylor Swift deciding whether to share her political views

Taylor Swift is an accomplished and successful singer songwriter in popular music, however her roots and early beginnings are in country music. She is a young female artist in the male-dominated music industry. The culture of country music is to keep politics out of your music. In 2018, Taylor's awareness was heightened around systemic injustices that routinely impact women and other groups when she won her court case after being sexually assaulted by a radio personality and was shaken by the entire experience. She noted that she likely received preferential treatment in court due to her celebrity. Taylor lamented how her situation could have played out for another woman who didn't have her fame, money and influence.

With an election coming up in her state, she felt compelled to speak out against a candidate whom she felt would deepen the powerlessness felt by many groups based on the policies the candidate promised to introduce.

Did I mention Taylor's musical roots and a large part of her fan base are in country music? Do you recall a group called the Dixie Chicks whose career came tumbling down after making disparaging comments about the sitting American president? The experience of the Dixie Chicks is a cautionary tale to anyone else who dares to veer out of their lane as an artist and lend their voice and support to specific political issues. There would also be security concerns about a fringe group of people who may strongly oppose her views and become threatening. The easiest, safest and most financially stable thing to do for Taylor would be to just shut up and sing.

There was much contemplation and debate amongst her team, most of whom agreed with her political views but feared the repercussions voicing them would have on her fan base. One advisor stated, "suppose we came to you saying we've got this idea that we could halve the number of people who would come to your next concert tour?"[11]

In the end, Taylor decided she was going to engage her fans and share her political views on the political issues around

Chapter 12: Principles Over Profits

human rights that she feels strongly about. Part of the decision is that she felt complicit by championing friends and fans who belong to groups that are marginalized and hurt by the same political policies being promoted by the candidate in her state. It felt disingenuous to champion them yet remain silent on the very real and visible attacks on their human rights.

Colin Kaepernick

Colin Kaepernick is one of the newest civil rights heroes. He is a talented football player who was first drafted into the NFL in 2011. Kaepernick started kneeling during the national anthem at the beginning of each football game in 2016 as a quiet protest about the racial injustice, systemic racism, and police brutality directed at African Americans. People seemed to either love and champion this quiet yet powerful protest or were deeply offended by it. The President of the United States at the time chose to interpret Colin's actions as disrespecting the country. He made disparaging comments about Kaepernick publicly and there is wide speculation that he strongly encouraged NFL owners, many of whom were the President's supporters, to blacklist Kaepernick by refusing to offer him a contract. Upon becoming a free agent in 2017, Colin was unable to secure a new football contract despite his impressive performance.

Colin never blinked. He had a brilliant future ahead of him in the NFL with the prospect of a financially lucrative career. His convictions about the need for change in America, however, meant more to him. In addition to his kneeling during the national anthem, Colin also contributed $1 million to a variety of organizations across the US that address racial injustice.[12] He inspired many other professional athletes to join his protests.

In September 2018, Nike launched a campaign featuring Colin with the tagline, "Believe in something. Even if it means sacrificing everything." The NFL eventually came to a settlement with Colin due to allegations of collusion against him.[13] Keep in mind that when Colin continued his protests, despite being unable to secure a contract, there was no line of sight to a Nike campaign or a settlement coming out of the NFL. He was acting on his values at the expense of his career.

How many people would sacrifice their livelihood and possibly lifetime earning potential for a principle or a cause they believe in?

Chapter 13:
High Trust Company Profile - Patagonia

I think Patagonia is badass. Patagonia doesn't try to keep up with progressive business strategies to protect the environment and enhance employee engagement. Patagonia is a trailblazer in this area unapologetically introducing radical programs to stay true to their values to protect the environment and create a supportive workplace for employees.

Yvon Choinard founded Patagonia in 1971 in Ventura, California. Yvon is an avid rock climber and Patagonia originally manufactured and sold rock climbing gear but later shifted to clothing for outdoor activities like skiing, hiking, surfing, cycling, and almost any other outdoor adventure you could imagine. The love for the outdoors was at the core of Yvon's motivation to create this company. Patagonia has remained true to its love for the outdoors ever since. In 2017, Utah Governor Gary Herbert lead a successful campaign to remove the protections put in place for the 1.35 million acres of land in Utah called Bears Ears which is home to some of the most spectacular landscapes in the US plus sacred land for some Native American tribes. Patagonia had participated in the Outdoor Show which was hosted in Utah for over 20 years where all major players in the outdoor industry display their latest gear and products. The show also brings the state multiple millions in tourist revenue. Patagonia pulled out of the show and successfully urged the Outdoor Industry Association, which organizes the exhibition, to seek a home for the exhibition in a state that values outdoor land.

Patagonia is consistent in thought, word and deed which has won itself a legion of rabid fans, I mean, customers.

What does Patagonia do?

Manufactures, markets and sells high quality outdoor clothing and gear in more than 10 countries around the world.

What is their position within the industry?

Patagonia is a privately held company so financial data isn't publicly available. We do know however that it has over $1 billion in annual sales.[1]

Why do we trust them – Reason #1

Support for employees living healthy, balanced lives

In his book ***Let My People Go Surfing***, Yvon Chouinard describes his philosophy, encouraging staff to take time to get into the outdoors to surf, hike or go biking. It's totally acceptable to partake of these activities in the middle of the workday, then make a quick clothing change and get back to work. Admittedly, it's also a great opportunity for employees to try out new gear and remain close to their adventurer clients. It also creates a great company culture where people can balance their stress with outdoor activities.

Support for Employees

Chapter 13: High Trust Company Profile - Patagonia

Patagonia employees can take a paid sabbatical of up to 2 months to work on an environmental project they are passionate about. Patagonia offers one of the most generous health care benefits to employees minimizing any out-of-pocket costs. There is also an onsite childcare program. "We support the whole community, as opposed to the few people who do very, very well and enjoy all the perks," noted Rose Marcario, CEO of Patagonia.[2]

Patagonia will pay for nannies to go on business trips. Many of their employees are environmental activists and Patagonia supports peaceful protesting. Should an employee find themselves in jail due to a protest, Patagonia will cover bail and legal costs for the employee and their partner. They do this because they want people to feel comfortable being themselves at work.

As a result, Patagonia has an employee turnover rate of 4% compared with their industry which is 13%.[3]

Why do we trust them – Reason #2
Fierce commitment to the environment

Patagonia is one of the loudest supporters of the environment by providing financial support for causes it believes in, as well as encouraging employees with paid time off to volunteer for their chosen environmental cause. Patagonia started to commit 1% of sales or 10% of profits (whichever is greater) to environmental causes in 1986.[4]

Choinard co-founded 1% for the Planet with Craig Matthews of Blue Ribbon Flies in 2002. The purpose of 1% for the Planet is to grow and nurture a community of companies that pledge 1% of gross sales to champion environmental causes.[5]

Why do we trust them – Reason #3
Patagonia's commitment to reducing consumerism – Patagonia's Worn Wear program
Repair, Share and recyle your gear

Patagonia is a clothing manufacturer committed to reducing consumerism. Sounds counter-intuitive however Patagonia believes we should purchase high quality clothing, which is what they make and sell, and keep them for the long term. When they get damaged, repair it. When you're finished with them, re-gift it. Send damaged clothing back to Patagonia and they'll repair them for you and return them. Send back used clothing and you'll get a credit towards a new purchase.

There are some inspiring, fun videos on YouTube under the name "Worn Wear" where Patagonia customers brag about the durability of their Patagonia gear. A hiker displays her shorts that have gotten her through 5,000 miles of hiking trails while another customer shows off his 9 year old Patagonia surf board. Repair, share and recycle your gear.

Chapter 14:
What Trust Is Not

Let's recall the story that opened this book. You'll remember that I lost my corporate innocence that Tuesday afternoon in October following the layoff of 15% of the organization. What's important to note is that layoffs don't trigger distrust in your employees. Layoffs happen and can be unfortunate for those impacted but can't be avoided over the lifetime of an organization with technology developments and changing business cycles. We are regularly alerted to some of the marketplace developments that are spurring distrust in employees and making them fear for their future. The migration of some jobs to lower cost markets globally. There's the shift from bricks and mortar establishments to doing business online. The pandemic accelerated this shift. Even when I go to some bricks and mortar retail outlets like my local grocery store, I'm over at the self-checkout lane rather than lining up for a human cashier. The growth of the world of artificial intelligence (AI) creates some concern for individuals who are not clear on how extensively it will be used. More specifically, the concern tends to center around the storage, use and access to the volume of personal data that is typically required as an input for AI processing.

My perspective is that we may fear the changes that these developments and innovations may introduce to our lives especially if we feel it may impact the security of our job or business. We may not understand how we, as professionals, will fit into the business world of the future however it doesn't trigger distrust. It may trigger uncertainty and discomfort. It could trigger worry and anxiety, but not distrust. Distrust is created by the actions of untrustworthy human beings.

Layoffs are sometimes used as a tool to improve financial results

Actions and events like layoffs don't create distrust within an organization. Distrust enters the room when, as we've seen over the last few decades, executives at large public companies use layoffs as a convenient tool to cut costs and hit financial targets which often boosts their own compensation. One of the most egregious examples was 2008, when the US government bailed out some of the largest banks on Wall Street who were on the verge of collapse in an effort to mitigate what many economists projected could have been a depression.

The US lost 2.6 million jobs in 2008[1] as a result of the economic downturn. At the end of 2008, nine of the financial institutions receiving bailout relief, waited for the funds to clear their accounts then collectively paid 5,000 of their traders and bankers more than $1 million each in bonuses.[2] I realize that compensation is a complex topic. Due to the employment and compensation contracts, it wasn't easy to legally withhold the bonuses. But let's take a giant step back. Big picture, your bank was on the brink of bankruptcy. The bank could have ceased to exist. It was so bad that it required your executives to turn to taxpayers begging for funds to stay afloat. It's relevant to point

Chapter 14: What Trust Is Not

out that it was the unscrupulous actions of some of those same banks that precipitated the financial crisis. How do you make a credible argument to say that all of those individuals produced results that were so outstanding when your institution was on the brink of insolvency? Clearly something is rotten in the state of their compensation structure. Some financial institutions returned the bonuses, but only after they were publicly called out. Returning the bonuses was less about finding their conscience but rather having your conscience delivered to them on the front page of every newspaper and as the headline story on every newscast every day.

This was a situation which gratefully rarely occurs, however the use of layoffs to boost corporate profits, shareholder value and executive bonuses has been a tactic which creates distrust that leaves employees feeling betrayed by organizations which talk routinely about how valuable their employees are.

I've observed that artificial intelligence (AI) is a technology advancement that makes some workers a bit nervous. There are stories woven about all humans being replaced in the workplace by super-efficient robots who never get tired, sick or grumpy. AI is one of the most transformational developments of our time. My Netflix recommendations make it clear that their algorithm knows me better than most of my family members. Rather than these recommendations making me feel distrustful, I appreciate them. Recommendations alerted me to "The Crown", "Hip Hop Evolution" and thanks to "Nadia Bakes," I now know how to make a vegan banana ice cream cheesecake. So why are people lobbying their governments to impose more regulations and closing their Facebook profiles (as if you can ever really delete your FB profile)?

Has Facebook protected their client's personal data?

Speaking of Facebook, they've been harshly criticized for capturing their client's data then sharing it with at least 150 companies. This client data can then be used to generate targeted marketing campaigns. There's a long list of the companies detailing the access they had in a New York Times article. At a high level, these companies could see the names of Facebook users, their friends and in some cases their personal messages, group chats and calendar items. This access was granted regardless of the privacy permissions that a user had set up on their FB profile. Many of the companies that were granted the data access indicated they weren't even aware of the level of access FB had granted them.

The issue here is that in 2011 FB promised the Federal Trade Commission that it would not share user data without their customers' explicit consent.

When called out, FB executives become defensive and are unable to clearly explain how and when data is shared in simple language everyone can understand. There's a complexity to their explanations that many interpret as a ploy to confuse the issue.

Note that one of the companies granted access is Yandex, head quartered in Russia. Russia has minimal to non-existent laws protecting the privacy of consumer data.[3]

So I think it's fair to say the distrust is triggered by dishonesty. Distrust is triggered by the actions of some of our business leaders who act in their own best interest at the expense of employees, clients and the larger stakeholder base reinforces the belief that we can't trust profit-driven corporations to act with integrity when there are financial gains to be made by looking the other way.

Chapter 15:
High Trust Company Profile - Salesforce

Salesforce is a company that I admire. This is a company with a big hairy audacious goal to create superior value for its clients while making the world a better place. Salesforce is bold enough to believe that those two goals can co-exist and, even better, reinforce each other.

Marc Benioff, the founder and CEO of Salesforce demonstrates a combination of confidence, business acumen, ambition as well as humility, self-awareness and compassion which is captured in great detail in his book ***Trailblazer: The power of business as the greatest platform for change.***

Salesforce has a well-deserved reputation of building a supportive, empowering environment for its employees in an intensely competitive and fast-paced industry. They have products, services and a relationship management approach that embraces their customers with a commitment to helping them to be successful in their respective marketplaces.

Finally, as the title of Marc's book describes, they want to be a platform for change in the world. They have an inspiring track record that shows this commitment. It's not all roses and sunflowers. They do stumble, as we all do sometimes. When these missteps happen, they are truly embraced as a moment for reflection and a catalyst for positive change.

What does Salesforce do?

Salesforce provides value for its clients by delivering a customer relationship management (CRM) tool which allows business people to keep track of customers and potential customers, identify sales opportunities and build their customer relationships.

What is Salesforce's standing in their industry?

Salesforce has a 19.5% market share for CRM tools with its nearest competitor a distant second place.[1]

Why do we trust them – Reason #1

Salesforce's commitment to pay equity

Salesforce has dedicated more than $8 million to ensuring that pay rates are equitable addressing inherent biases across gender, race and ethnicity.[2]

In chapter 6 of ***Trailblazer***, Benioff details the challenge in addressing pay equity in a meaningful way. It starts with recognizing there's a problem. Two of his female senior team members brought the issue to his attention showing him that there were significant pay discrepancies of individuals doing the same jobs. The bottom line was that women and visible minorities were paid at the lower end of the scale. They diligently conducted a pay audit and took action to bring up the pay of those who were lagging below their colleagues. What Marc and his team soon realized is that this is not a one-time fix.

Chapter 15: High Trust Company Profile - Salesforce

In addition to the unconscious bias of hiring managers, there were also behaviour differences that saw some employees starting the salary negotiation with lower pay expectations. Some employees were less likely to proactively request raises. These and other factors meant that addressing pay equity isn't a "one-and-done" fix but something the organization would need to monitor going forward to adjust for these other factors that drive variances in compensation.

Why do we trust them – Reason #2
Commitment to treating employees and clients as family

The Hawaiian concept of "family" known as "Ohana" is at the core of Salesforce's corporate values.

Benioff describes the "Ohana" principle and how it is woven through the Salesforce culture in great detail in chapter 7 of **Trailblazer**. He deeply believes in treating his employees, clients and the communities they serve as close relatives. Each employee is given seven paid days each year to volunteer for a not-for profit of their choice. They run a "Becoming Salesforce" bootcamp on a campground where executives share expectations and strategies to be successful within the company. New hires are welcomed into the Salesforce "family". Camp B-Well is a program where experts are brought in to educate the staff on the pillars of healthy living by nutritional experts, sleep experts, and others. Salesforce demonstrates that they care about their employees living healthy, successful lives inside and outside of the office.

Why do we trust them – Reason #3
Mistakes are used as a catalyst for reflection and positive change

On July 9, 2016 Benioff tweeted what he intended to be a comment supporting Black Lives Matter activist DeRay Mckesson, who was arrested wearing a t-shirt representing Black Birds, a resource group for African Americans employees within the Twitter organization. Benioff's tweet "amazing to see tech as a vehicle for social change. Respect" was not well-received as respondents pointed out that the technology industry has a horrible track record for hiring Black people. Someone shared a tweet showing that the employee base at Facebook, Twitter and Salesforce was no more than 2% Black. It was a turning point for Benioff who "looked in the mirror" and decided it was time to make diversity and equality an organizational priority. He hired a Chief Equality Officer to provide leadership on the company strategy. They made partnerships with colleges and organizations that support the training and education of underserved communities. Through their Futureforce initiative, they have focused on hiring diverse candidates from universities, youth programs, veterans and their spouses with 43% of new hires in 2018 coming from these groups.

Benioff states that although he's remorseful of the hurt that his insensitive tweet caused, he is deeply grateful for it and the controversy that ensued as it woke him up and was a catalyst for change within Salesforce.

… PART 2

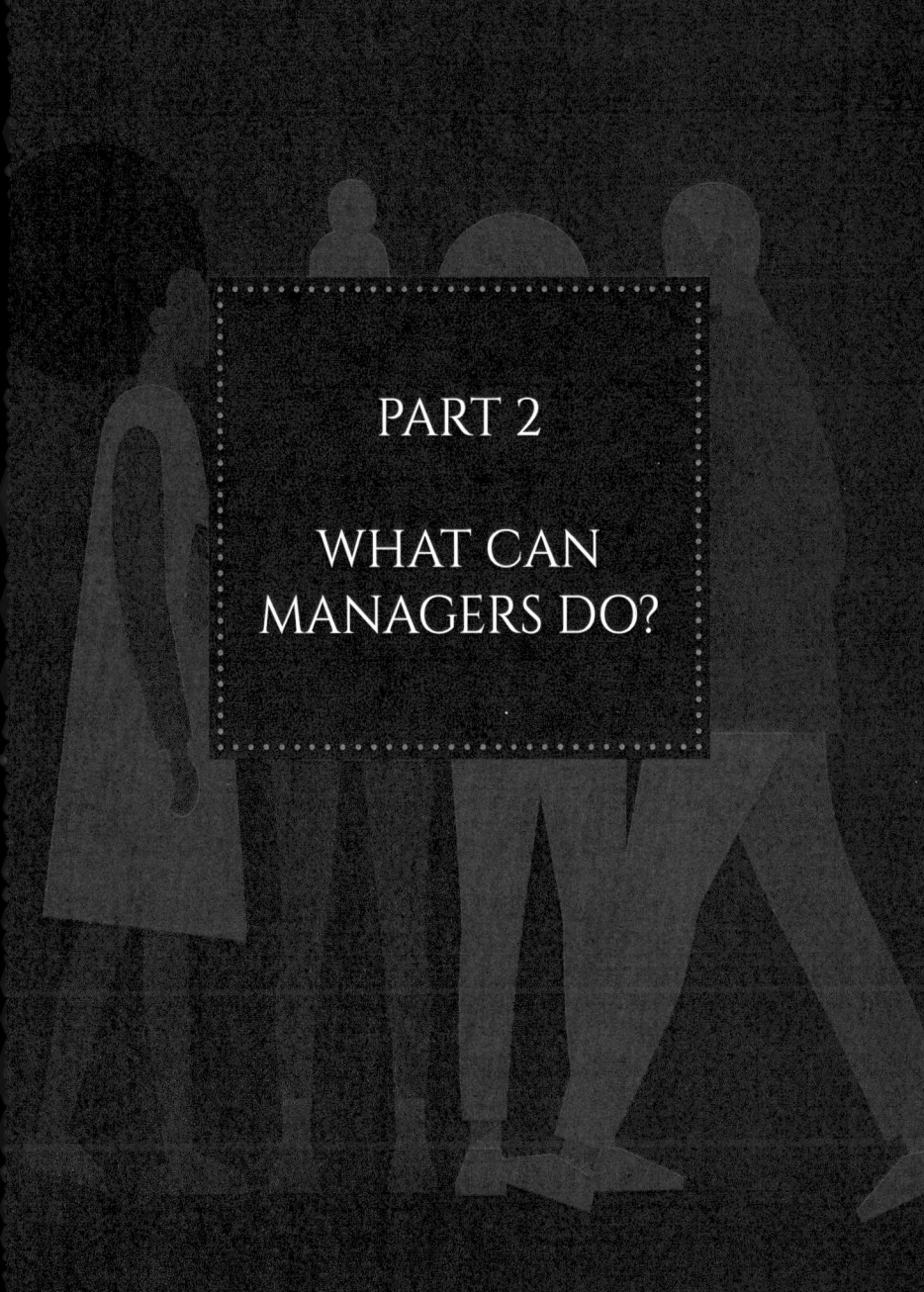

WHAT CAN MANAGERS DO?

Chapter 16:
Give trust first

Pastor Bruce Deel with the help of Sara Grace wrote the heartwarming book "Trust First: A True Story About the Power of Giving People Second Chances". This book tells the story of Pastor Deel, his family and his team who took over a church in an area of Atlanta, Georgia that was overridden with poverty, crime and homelessness. Most assumed he would close down the church within weeks of arriving. Instead, they renamed the church the City of Refuge. This church has been so successful in assisting neighbourhood residents to improve their station in life that the City of Refuge model has been replicated across the US and Pastor Deel is regularly requested to share his process with other organizations trying to impact meaningful change in their communities.

The City of Refuge was successful by exercising "radical trust". The book is filled with personal stories of how the Pastor and his team started by demonstrated trust in the people they were trying to help. They put trust in people that society would label as the least trustworthy individuals in society. I've already shared that his program was phenomenally successful and the extreme trust they put in people is a foundational element of their success formula.

Chapter 16: Give trust first

Were there some people who didn't reciprocate the trust? Of course. However the reality is that the vast majority of people rose up to the trust that was bestowed on them.

Trust is a risk leaders have to take

Simon Sinek shared a similar perspective on his YouTube Channel in a video entitled "Trust your Teams" which he recorded September 2021. In the video he asserts that "Trusting is one of the risks a leader has to take. The more we give trust, the more we receive trust in return. And if we give people a sense of control and autonomy, we end up with healthier, happier teams."

Taking this into a business context, I would acknowledge that the radical trust that Pastor Deel exercised so expertly would need to be modified. In the business world we need to have a level of control and governance. We need to make sure that if you said you sold 3 widgets, three widgets were actually sold. We need to get our financial statements audited first internally then by an external accounting firm. All of these controls ensure that there are no gaps in our business process and our reporting is accurate for our investors and our regulators.

Where Pastor Deel's approach is most applicable is when it comes to the management of our teams. As Simon states, a leader needs to trust first. Managers need to treat their team members as responsible adults who are capable of delivering on their responsibilities. Demonstrate your faith in individuals and most will rise to the occasion.

I'm someone who trusts almost to a fault. But that's intentional. That's just who I want to be in the world. No one will ever accuse me of micromanagement or hoarding work. As a result of this approach I have been disappointed by team members on occasion. I've felt let down, possibly even betrayed and sometimes there's a voice in the back of my head that urges me to trust less. But then I remind myself that the vast majority of people reciprocate the trust that I put in them and demonstrate that I was wise to trust them and help them to grow, take on more responsibility and feel empowered.

As long as far more people demonstrate they are trustworthy than those who fall short, you're doing fine. When we trust, there are no guarantees that everyone will fall in line. The alternative of always being distrustful of others is just not in alignment with who I am as a person. I can't walk around looking over my shoulder all the time. I believe that most people are good and want to do well and its our role as a manager to help them to realize that potential.

Chapter 17:
How Managers Can Foster Trust With Their Teams

Trust is "the basis for almost everything we do as civilized people" argues Frances Frei and Anne Morris in their HBR article "Begin with Trust". They share that trust is "one of the most essential forms of capital a leader has." That sounds like a tall order.

Grab your popcorn and get comfortable because in this chapter we get to the core of the purpose of this book. Here, we share strategies to assist managers in fostering trust with team members, colleagues, leaders and customers.

Managers are the linchpins in organizations, and play a critical role in building trust. The executive team can come up with the most brilliant strategies but if managers are not able to engage, mobilize and optimize the production of their teams, the organization will only achieve modest results and leave lots of opportunity on the table.

The ability to gain the trust of team members is a critical skill to getting team members engaged and available to do their best work.

Academics have been studying organizational trust for decades. Researchers explore the many roles that trust plays in business. How do we build trust? How do we maintain trust? How do we repair trust when it's broken? Trust between co-workers. Trust in the manager-employee relationship. Trust between organizations. These are just a handful of topics covered in the expansive scope of trust research.

In their research paper "Measuring trust in organizational research", Professors Bill

McEvily and Marco Tortoreillo et al assessed the various measurements and tools that were being used at the time to assess the trustworthiness of business leaders. They tallied that across all the tools there were 38 attributes that were being used to identify high trust leaders. Ability, benevolence and integrity were the top three attributes that were most widely referenced in trust measurement tools. Let's take a look at how these three attributes factor into building trusting relationships as a leader.

The ability to get the job done

Simply put, does your team believe you are capable to lead them to success? Do you have the right technical skills to understand and execute your role? If not, are you able to learn quickly on the job? Do you effectively leverage the skills and knowledge of team members and colleagues to arrive at solutions? Are you able to build productive, collaborative working relationships with your peers across the organization? Are you effective at organizing the team in a manner to optimize their contribution? Are you decisive? Do you have a backbone? When the

Chapter 17: How Managers Can Foster Trust With Their Teams

team hits a roadblock they aren't able to manage themselves, are you able to help facilitate a solution?

This is the short list of the many things your team needs you to be able to do to help them to deliver a quality output and achieve success. If you also spring for lunch once in a while and purchase a round of drinks every so often, you're golden. Under the category of Ability, consider you'll need technical ability, the ability to build strong relationships and finally understand how to get things done through your team.

Technical Ability

Some managers are promoted into the leadership role after working their way up through more junior roles. You may not have experienced the fairy tale of starting in the mailroom and working your way up to the position of CEO. Your experience may look more like, Junior Analyst, Senior Analyst, Manager, Senior Manager and now head of the department. This experience gives you first-hand knowledge to not just understand what the team does, but understand why they do things a particular way. This insight is useful for designing strategy and making meaningful recommendations on changes. It also gives you instant credibility as a subject matter expert. There is, however, a downside to learning as you come up through the ranks.

Sometimes we are too close to how we do things and unwittingly find ourselves in an invisible box we can't see that limits what we consider to be in the realm of the possible.

This is the reason why managers are sometimes moved around. The Director of Finance takes a lateral move into Operations. He may not be familiar with the technical details of operations however he has his leadership skills which are transferable. The operations lead in a grocery store chain may take a job as the head of operations in a toy distribution company. She has subject matter expertise in operations but would be on a learning curve when it comes to her knowledge of the toy industry. In these situations, you bring a strong background of success however you're light on specific technical skills for this new role. You just need a good plan to come up your learning curve quickly. This technical knowledge will be critical to winning the confidence of your team and having the full context to frame decisions, problems and strategy. The fact that you're not instantly a subject matter expert on how things are done in your new team means that you're also not limited by existing ways of doing things. You can bring a fresh perspective on challenges and opportunities.

Ability to build strong business relationships

The team needs to trust that you are able to build productive, collaborative working relationships with your colleagues. They need the confidence that you can broker compromises and solutions with your peers across the organizations. Your team may be running behind on their timeline because they're waiting for a critical report from marketing. Their colleagues in marketing are not ignoring them, it's just that there are three other items that are ranked as a higher priority so your team's request ranks number four on their priority list. Your team needs you to reach out to your peer in marketing to see if you can negotiate getting the report bumped up or help to find an alternate solution. They need for you to have a good working relationship with your peer in marketing or the ability to forge a productive business relationship.

If you aren't able to effectively work collaboratively with your peers or, your team doesn't think you can, the team is left to

Chapter 17: How Managers Can Foster Trust With Their Teams

try to influence the prioritization from bottom up which can work but is not a good use of their time and leaves them feeling unsupported. If they believe you can't be trusted to play nicely in the sandbox with your peers, or worse, you have a reputation for making matters worse, they will work around you. You will become yet another challenge they need to work around rather than a trusted, supportive leader. It's unfortunate, but I've encountered more than a handful of leaders whose teams effectively worked around them.

It's also critical that you will hold peers accountable. When things go sideways, the team needs to know that you aren't afraid to have a direct, possibly difficult conversation to get issues resolved.

Ability to get things done through your team

Genius level intellect and being effective in your role are not inextricably intertwined. When leaders are both brilliant and effective it's a magical combination. I've learned so much from these double threat leaders. Then we have the leaders who are far more profound than practical. Profound is intriguing at a cocktail party but rarely gets things done. Remember, getting things done through people is a very specific skill set we need in our people managers. It's not necessarily intuitive.

Simply, there are activities the team needs to be doing every day in order to move the organization towards its goals. The specific activities differ depending on role and industry but the fundamental truth is the same whether you manage workers on a manufacturing assembly line or manage the internal communications for an organization. In some roles, unexpected priorities pop up all the time and need to be addressed but anything that prevents team members from consistently performing their core activities will impact their ability to deliver what the organization needs for everyone to be successful and meet their monthly, quarterly and annual goals. On a really basic level, managers need to maximize the amount of time their teams have to focus on those key activities that produce the output the company needs to win.

I recall a big hearted, passionate leader whose head and heart were in the right place. He was a fairly senior executive whose people management experience was mainly managing individual contributors and consultants. He had never led a large operations team and definitely not a team directly supporting external clients. He took on a new operations leadership role with passion and enthusiasm. He was obsessed with simplifying the work-life for the teams that interact directly with clients to improve the client experience. He would spend every Monday morning visiting a front office location and capture any grievances they shared with a commitment to getting it resolved by his head office team. He would commit to investigating and fixing every single issue raised. He also implored them to email him if any other issues came up. He was engaged, motivated and responsive.

I was a member of his head office team and we braced ourselves each Monday for an onslaught of issues that all had to be investigated and resolved within the timeline he had promised which was ASAP (as soon as possible). Each week was peppered with issues needing a resolution. They were urgent, frequent and unexpected. I totally got it. I would never argue with a focus on optimizing the client experience and simplifying life for those who directly serve our clients. This system worked brilliantly except for one issue. Our head office team had our own major projects and initiatives with tight timelines. The

Chapter 17: How Managers Can Foster Trust With Their Teams

big-hearted leader's heart sank at the realization that a number of initiatives would be delayed.

How?

Why?

Turns out having urgent issues randomly drop on your desks daily is one of the most effective ways to throw well laid plans off course.

It would have been more effective to have a handful of team members designated as a SWAT team dedicated to investigating and resolving these urgent issues while the rest of the team could focus consistently on the larger initiatives. Admittedly, the entire team could probably be described as a handful of team members so there wasn't a meaningful opportunity to break us into sub-groups. Perhaps we could have managed the expectations around the turnaround times and implement a form of triaging the issues to determine the priority so that the issues could be addressed while still allowing the structure needed to progress and complete our core initiatives.

It's a skill to understand how to manage a team of people to advance the strategy while remaining responsive. Problems always pop up and they need to be addressed without bringing the entire assembly line to a halt. It's a skill to understand how your actions can unintentionally make it harder not easier for the team to get shit done.

Be benevolent

It warms my heart to see concepts like benevolence taking its rightful place at the center of effective leadership skills. Regardless of what you may have heard, I'm a benevolent person at heart. I believe the best way to achieve success is to help others to be successful. I whole-heartedly believe most people are good, well-meaning and want to show up each day as productive team members. As I point out in my first book **Thrive Despite the Assholes@Work** sometimes we unintentionally frustrate our colleagues.

There is never any confusion about why we all show up at work daily. When we joined the organization, we fully understood that we signed up to advance the organization's mandate and create value for our clients. Those goals are not negotiable. There was no section in our employment contract that promised us self-actualization, inner-peace and a perfect balance between our responsibilities at home and work.

Strong leaders understand that within the corporate mandate, there's lots of room to help our team members achieve their goals, be more effective and lower their stress.

Interestingly, and not surprisingly, some of the most productive teams I've worked with had benevolent leaders. When people know that you genuinely care about them and have their back, this fosters loyalty and the motivation to go above and beyond to support the team. There's a reciprocal relationship between strong leaders and their teams.

What's really important to your team members?

Do you know what your team members' professional dreams are? A leader I've worked with who has a strong track record for developing high performing teams makes a point of making this topic part of her performance discussions. If she inherits a new team or hires someone new, she makes sure to find out where they would ideally like to go professionally. She's great at building rapport and fostering trust such that most people

Chapter 17: How Managers Can Foster Trust With Their Teams

are comfortable sharing their professional dreams even if their goals mean their stint on her team is just a temporary stepping stone. That's totally fine with her. When you're here, the expectation is that you'll perform and if she can assist in any way, introducing them to people in the organization who could help on their path, she's happy to do so. For her, the biggest disadvantage to her leadership style is that her team is regularly poached for talent by other areas in the organization.

Another leader who is equally effective has a completely different style. He finds more casual opportunities to get to know his team members and understand who they are beyond their resume and Linked In profile. He asks about their weekend. Inquires about their interests. He'll start a coaching session with some casual banter. He probes to find common interests like sports, books or maybe his love of good food or his extensive knowledge of rum. He learns that for some team members spending as much time as possible with their kids is their number one focus. Another team member may be pursuing her masters degree part-time. This knowledge allows him to understand what motivates his team members and allows him to build a stronger bond as they learn that he truly cares about their ability to be successful human beings as well as productive members of his team. These leaders are rarely surprised when a team member resigns because they probably already gave him a heads up and he was likely one of their references for the new role.

Radical Candor, written by Kim Malone Scott is filled with sage advice on building trust as a leader. Kim shares that "probably the most important thing you can do to build trust is to spend a little time alone with each of your direct reports on a regular basis". This is an opportunity to get to know them and foster a strong professional relationship.

This caring approach, if it's sincere, generates professional dividends in the form of higher loyalty rates and commitment to going over and beyond for the team. These leaders are comfortable that not everyone dreams of working for them for the rest of their lives and they are totally cool with that.

Despite the tangible business benefits of demonstrating that you care about your team, managers that I would describe as benevolent primarily do it because they are simply benevolent human beings who enjoy seeing others thrive and succeed.

Be Kind

Our lives are incredibly busy. The COVID-19 pandemic has put a spotlight on what has been true for years. In addition to meeting grueling timelines, many of us have significant responsibilities outside of work. Parenting children, caring for elderly family members or perhaps completing a challenging educational program part time. Some of us go through a particularly stressful period dealing with an illness or other traumatic life experience. Issues we may be dealing with ourselves or assisting someone close to us with include but are not limited to: chronic illness, terminal illness, divorce, death, miscarriage, depression, addiction, abusive relationships, eating disorders, financial challenges, etc. This isn't a random list of potential issues. Every single one of the issues above have been experienced by people I've managed over the years where they have felt comfortable to share them with me and I have had to manage a few of them personally.

My experience is that the team members who shared some of these incredibly stressful situations with me, had no

Chapter 17: How Managers Can Foster Trust With Their Teams

distinguishing characteristics than any of their peers. They didn't have an emoji on their shirt signaling their mood. They are professionals who maintained their performance level. I would have never known if they didn't disclose their situation to me. Correspondingly, there are also folks living their best life on any given day.

I share this to make the point that each day we show up at work we don't know what our colleagues are dealing with. The suggestion is simple. Don't be an asshole. There's enough stress due to the routine pressures of our work. People don't need the added stress of dealing with an immature and insensitive manager. Pettiness, moodiness, spitefulness, dishonesty, game-playing are a handful of the many toxic behaviours that are unnecessary, unhelpful and unwanted in our managers. "If you can choose to be anything in life, choose to be kind". We wear the t-shirt. I see you posting the memes on your social media page. Let's live it each day.

Be guided by integrity

Trust and integrity are linked. I can't imagine a situation where I trust someone whom I would describe as lacking integrity. Integrity is about having a set of values that you stay true to no matter what. I am a huge fan of Gary Vaynerchuk. He's an entrepreneur and author. He shares that his father taught him one of his most valuable life lessons. His father said that "your word is bond". Having the reputation of being true to your word was valuable 200 years ago, it's true today and will be true 200 years from now. Be known for honouring your word. I am grateful to have some individuals in my life whom I know that once they say they are going to do something, it's as good as done. I don't need to ask them a second time or follow up.

What does integrity mean in a leadership context?

Integrity means following through on your commitments regardless of whether they are documented and signed by a notary and witnessed by a judge or if it was a promise made passing someone in the hallway. Sometimes we need to back out of a commitment. When you value your word, backing out of a commitment is done only after serious contemplation once all alternatives have been exhausted.

Being transparent helps us build our reputation for integrity. If you say you will support a colleague's project in a meeting, then you follow through. If you tell your team it's okay to contact you after hours for urgent issues, you make yourself available. If you say the meeting will only last 15 minutes, you're happy when people give you a time check at 14 min and 30 seconds to remind you it's time to wrap things up. New information may arise causing you to change your position at which point, you let people know.

Being transparent helps us to build our reputation for acting with integrity. Share as much information about the company, decision-making and strategic decisions as possible. Sure, there are confidential topics. You're not going to discuss compensation and the performance ratings of other team members or a highly sensitive strategic decision that's pending. But that still leaves a broad range of information that is available for sharing. This allows your team to consider you a credible source of information. They can trust you to deliver praise and share opportunities as well as constructive criticism and bad news.

Chapter 17: How Managers Can Foster Trust With Their Teams

Do people trust that you hire the most qualified and best suited candidates for roles or, is there a belief that you are hiring those who are loyal to you or worse, relatives or friends regardless of their competency for the role?

Are you seen to make the best decisions for the organization or do people believe you are always guided to make the decision that is the most beneficial to you personally?

Our integrity forces us to make the best decision for the organization even if it disadvantages us in the short run. Is there a high level of transparency within the organization? Are the leaders perceived to have a strong moral and ethical compass? Employees may not agree with every decision but is there a belief that leaders are focused on making decisions that are in the best interest of the longevity of the organization and its ability to increase its value proposition to clients over the long run?

Can profit-driven organizations be trusted to do the right thing?

There's a prevalent belief that profit-maximizing organizations can't be relied on to self-regulate and exercise integrity. Won't they always choose the most profitable option regardless of the impact? I would like to resoundingly denounce this belief but there are so many high-profile examples of corporations throwing integrity out the window in order to make a few extra bucks. I am, however, filled with hope that this is changing.

Trust is not a destination we arrive at and get a badge, certificate or degree freeing us up to move on to tackle another organizational challenge. Trust is a little like having a great lawn. If your lawn is overrun by weeds and brown patches, it will take a lot of work over a few seasons to get rid of the weeds and brown spots and plant fresh grass seed, water and mow to help rejuvenate the lawn. It will be an intensive effort.

But once you have a lawn that's the envy of the neighbourhood, maintenance is still required. The maintenance will be less effort than what was required to bring it from a parched, dried out patch to a dazzling green healthy lawn, but regular maintenance is needed. A few weeds may pop up or a dry patch but if caught quickly, it can be rectified swiftly before it becomes a larger problem.

Trust is like a beautiful green lawn; it takes a while to create, and needs ongoing maintenance to prevent it from disappearing.

Here are some additional strategies managers can use to build trust with their teams.

Transparency and Openness

Share as much as you can as often as possible. "If there is a void of information, employees will fill it and they will always fill it with negative information," says Jim Dougherty, software executive and senior lecturer at MIT Sloan School of Management.[1]

There are situations that call for discretion and confidentiality rather than transparency and openness. We won't share details like the details of a team member's performance review, annual bonus or strategy considerations that could impact other employees. Putting those topics aside, you're left with the majority of daily and weekly information to share. You want to be your team's "go to" person for accurate, credible information. This minimizes the value of the grapevine as a credible source of what's going on. When rumours pop up, as they always do,

Chapter 17: How Managers Can Foster Trust With Their Teams

your team members will feel comfortable knowing they can come to you to get the facts.

How do we manage confidential information?

But suppose the rumour is that a division of the organization will be outsourced resulting in job losses. You deny knowing anything about it because it's true and it's also currently confidential. What happens three months later when the truth of the outsourcing is confirmed including the upcoming job losses? How do you retain your trust with your employees? Simple. When it becomes public, you re-visit it with the individuals who asked you about it and explain that your modus operandi is always to be open and honest however given the sensitivity of the initiative, you needed to maintain confidentiality until all the analysis was complete and ready to share. This was necessary to protect those who may have been impacted by this change. When you have a team of mature adults, they understand this. It's helpful if you have a track record of openness and transparency to back you up. If a team member doesn't accept your explanation and interprets your denial of the rumour as a betrayal, that's unfortunate however it's clear they're not ready for leadership. That would be an opportunity for you to provide them with some coaching.

To effectively exercise openness and transparency, you also need to demonstrate discretion. Having information about layoffs leak prior to all the preparations being completed is disastrous. I was involved in the damage control after a leak about an employee's layoff. It was an honest but sloppy mistake by the individual preparing the packages for individuals being laid off. He accidentally copied the employee on the email to his manager to clarify the details. The organization had to scramble to ensure the individual had all the details they needed including HR and counselling support on a Friday night that kicked off a 3-day long weekend. In addition to the potential legal and reputational risk for the organization, think about how the employee felt all weekend after finding out accidentally they were being laid off as the details were still being finalized.

The good news here is that unless you're a member of the Canadian Joint Task Force or a Navy Seal, highly confidential initiatives is not a weekly occurrence so most information is available for sharing.

At weekly touchpoints share the latest from your management update. What decisions were made and why were they made? What's the area of focus right now? What's going well? Where are we struggling? Providing this context does a few things.

It brings the team into the loop and gives them a temperature check on what's going on. Knowledge of the organizational priorities helps your team to prioritize their work and make decisions that are in alignment with these priorities. It helps them to be more independent. It's key to engagement so we feel like trusted partners as opposed to cogs in a wheel following instructions to execute someone else's strategy, until the metaphorical whistle blows at 5 PM. Some of you will remember the cartoon **The Flinstones** when the whistle blew at the quarry where Fred Flinstone and Barney Rubble worked, they were "outta there," zooming off in what was likely a pretty hot car by stone age standards.

Chapter 17: How Managers Can Foster Trust With Their Teams

Communication that's honest, tactful and direct

Kim Scott wrote in the revised version of her book **Radical Candor** of her disappointment after realizing that the HBO series "Silicon Valley" did a parody of the original edition of **Radical Candor**. They mocked the term "radical candor" as a cover for obnoxious behaviour by some shady leaders. She speaks in the preface to the revised edition that some would hide obnoxious and aggressive behaviour behind the shield of being "radically candid", with leaders shrugging their shoulders and proclaiming that they're "just keeping it real." If they actually read **Radical Candor**, especially the revised edition, they would find it speaks extensively about compassion and building trust.

Similar to the commentary around transparency where I note that discretion is just as important as openness and transparency, editing ourselves and deciding what is best left unsaid is just as important as candor. I filter my comments, particularly those that could be perceived as critical, through the lens of "intent". What is my intention in sharing this information? Is it useful to the recipient? Will something change for the better upon my sharing? If I find myself wanting to say something just to "get it off my chest", "give someone a piece of my mind", "tell them about themselves" or enlighten them to the "error of their ways", it's probably best I have some valerian root tea and try a few yoga poses instead to get it out of my system. Our egos are strong characters. My ego has been in the driver seat for many of my poor decisions. Exercise self-awareness and understand your motivation in providing the planned feedback.

Once we do a self-scan to ensure that our intentions are well-meaning for the recipient, then we can move forward with honest, tactful and direct communication. If you're sharing some constructive feedback, you can set the framework by sharing that you've grown in your development by leaders taking the time to share similar observations with you and you continue that practice.

Provide context for decisions

In their book ***Extreme Ownership***, Jacko Willink and Leif Babin share a situation where a leader rolled out a new compensation program for the sales team. Her sales managers were resistant to the change, expecting that most of their salespeople would dislike the change and potentially leave to work for their competitors. The sales managers were beside themselves. Apart from the obvious motivation to save money, the sales managers were perplexed why the company would cut costs in a manner that could have such a substantial impact to the sales team and their motivation to drive sales.

Their leader hadn't explained the strategy behind the compensation changes. She hadn't shared that she was aware that a few salespeople may leave. She articulated the bigger picture of how it would make the company more competitive and would likely increase the take home pay of the stronger sales people referencing a similar strategy she successfully executed at another company. Once she took the time to explain the rationale behind the changes, the managers understood why the changes were necessary and were now able to confidently roll it out and address challenges that came their way.[2] People need to understand the reason behind a change before they can fully support it, particularly if it could negatively impact them.

Chapter 17: How Managers Can Foster Trust With Their Teams

The leader should have taken the time to properly explain the change and the underlying rationale to get everyone on the same page. The managers who were struggling to understand and support the changes should have put their hand up and raised their concerns.

If someone did a great job, tell them and be clear about the specific action they took. If you think their deliverable fell short of your expectations and/or what you believe they are capable of, tell them. Employ tact. We're not killing off an opponent in Fortnite. The intent is to coach not crush. You need your team members to trust you equally when you are praising them as when you're providing constructive feedback.

Commander's Intent

I first heard about "the commander's intent" in the book ***Made to Stick*** by Chip Heath and Chris Heath. It's a concept adopted from the military where, much like most corporations, there's often a slew of communications that leaders need to read on a daily basis. The military employed a tactic whereby at the beginning of a communication the commander's intent would be listed in simple language at the top. It would identify the objective of the communication to ensure that the intention of the communication doesn't get lost. The intent may be, "option to complete implementation by Friday" or "plan to reduce overtime by 10%." Now everyone is clear on what we're trying to accomplish. Without the clear intent, it's easy for someone to be well intentioned and stray from the objective. If it isn't clear that the intent is "option to complete implementation by Friday", a team member may come up with an alternate solution that would save 5% on costs but wouldn't be delivered until next Monday. Great, but that wasn't the intention. It also eliminates the time people spend trying to figure out what the objective is or go down a road that has merits but doesn't achieve the intended goal. An added benefit is that it gives those charged with executing the instructions with more latitude on how they fulfill the Commander's Intent. If an option is uncovered to more effectively deliver on the task, the team is empowered to pursue that new option.

Employing the "commanders intent" is an opportunity to for a leader to empower their team with the information and context to subsequently set them up for success.

Truly Listen

Would it be condescending to state the obvious that we have two ears and just one mouth? It's basic but sometimes we need regular reminders. At times, I fall into the trap of believing my job as the manager to have the answers. I am uncomfortable with silent pauses and would be quick to fill dead air with words. Not necessarily useful or meaningful words, but enough words to fill the gap. When I shut up and listen, even through what could be very expressive periods of silence, I learn far more and recognize that I don't have all or even the best solutions.

How often does your team proactively share information and opinions with you without being asked? That's a great gauge about their level of trust in you. In Bernard T. Ferrari's book **Power Listening**, he states that team members need to feel comfortable that you are open to hearing their input and know that it will be given serious consideration. A strategy he suggests is to use a phrase like "talking to you always helps my thinking" and adopt a mindset that you could hear something that will be helpful. This strategy delivered sincerely can be effective.

Chapter 17: How Managers Can Foster Trust With Their Teams

When you sincerely listen and accept input and feedback, your team will feel more comfortable being forthcoming with their ideas and suggestions. If you just say things like "I'm here to listen" without a track record of being receptive to input, the team will perceive this to be a sound bite that sounds nice but they won't venture to share their input.

The inspiring speaker who listened more than he spoke

In his book ***The Power of Giving Away Power***, Matthew Barzun, former US Ambassador to the United Kingdom and Sweden, shares an insightful story about listening. Barzun had arranged a fundraiser for then-senator Obama, who was running for the leadership of the Democratic party in 2008, the first step ultimately towards becoming the President of the United States. Matthew arranged a high-priced fundraiser in Louisville, Kentucky for Obama. Obama's next appointment was delayed and he asked Barzun if he could round up anyone who couldn't make it to the high-priced event for a more intimate discussion. Obama was looking for a cross-section of individuals from different political affiliations for a good discussion on the pressing issues the country is facing. Barzun recalls that Obama spoke very little but rather went around the table asking attendees to share what was on their mind and their feelings on what the country needed. He would then paraphrase back to them to ensure he captured their comments accurately.

What surprised Barzun was the feedback he received after the event. Multiple attendees relayed to him that they thought Obama was an "inspiring speaker who lit up the room." Barzun found this ironic as Obama mostly listened and paraphrased.

Barzun later summarized that Obama, in fact, lit up the room, but not with his own light. He lit up the room by paying attention and listening to each participant, each person actually got lit up and everyone collectively lit up the room. Obama said relatively little yet the experience of the participants was that he was inspiring and lit up the room because he took the time to listen to them.[3]

We must be accountable

Accountability is an attribute that is celebrated in corporate mission statements and core values. We promise that we will hold ourselves and everyone else accountable. Even clients are held accountable for behaviours like treating our team members with respect. I think accountability is critical for maintaining a successful and empowering culture. So many of these principles are linked and reinforce each other. Accountability is definitely inter-connected with many of the other attributes like fairness, admitting our mistakes and candor. You can't have trust without having a habit of holding ourselves and others accountable. Here's what accountability can look like in action.

I was on a challenging project with multiple, diverse stakeholders and it was time to make a big strategic decision on how to move forward. The project was pivotal to the organization's growth projections and we were facing a key decision on the approach we were going to adopt.

Of course, the proper research and analysis was conducted and there would be comprehensive discussions with all the relevant partners to capture their input. But once all relevant information was gathered and shared, it was time to make a decision. Cheryl was the lead on the project and was a skilled

Chapter 17: How Managers Can Foster Trust With Their Teams

practitioner at holding people accountable. She needed the agreement of the seven stakeholders. Due to scheduling challenges, she had met with them in groups of two or three and gained agreement to move ahead with Plan A. Time was of the essence and we had one last stakeholder to meet with. Two of the others stakeholders who had already confirmed Plan A joined the meeting to assist with the discussion and help drive towards confirming a decision. The last stakeholder started asking about other options we had already discussed and dismissed as inferior options. We shared the team's feedback on those other options and why they were deemed to be less favourable, then, right before our eyes, the two stakeholders who came along to offer support and aid in the discussion to close out this final decision maker, started wavering as well, again, on options we had already discussed.

Modeling how to hold others accountable

Cheryl halted the discussion and reminded her two peers about the critical nature of this decision and our need to move forward. She then outlined all the steps that were taken to gather all the relevant information and speak to those who needed to be engaged. She said this was time to make a decision and if people were going to continue to re-open old discussions, we will fail.

It was less of a "pep talk" and more of a "stop fucking around" moment. She was professional and respectful but she was also unapologetic in holding her colleagues accountable for their role and responsibility on the project. A decision needed to be made. We would win together or fail together. If new information comes up, sure, let's stop and talk about it, but we were discussing leftovers from last week.

That was a defining moment for the project. We closed out the decision within two days and moved on to implement a successful project that rendered a number of impressive business results. As other decisions came up the message was clear. We will diligently gather and assess the information we need and engage the relevant folks in a robust discussion on the path forward. But once that was over, we were making decisions. Cheryl held the team accountable for their role as decision makers and was a valuable role model for the rest of us on the team.

Strong leaders hold their teams accountable for their commitments. Team members can trust that everyone is held to the same standard. Not only will we deliver on time, but what we deliver will be high quality. As a team member my responsibility is not just to deliver but also to put my hand up if I'm having a challenge or running behind and ask for the help that I need.

Finally, it undermines trust when a leader doesn't understand that accountability works both ways. Strong leaders hold themselves to the same standard as everyone else and sometimes a higher standard. If they make a mistake, they are the first to put up their hand and own it.

Show appreciation

Thank you is one of the least expensive and most impactful forms of appreciation. A thank you takes many forms. It could be a simple, sincere verbal expression of thanks. It may be sent as an email, arrive handwritten on a note card or even a cup of coffee. It demonstrates that you are paying attention and noticed the effort and are taking the time to acknowledge it.

The thank you should be sincere. There's sometimes a thought that, well, that's your job, why do I need to thank

Chapter 17: How Managers Can Foster Trust With Their Teams

you? I'm often surprised when norms in our everyday lives are opposite to what we practice in the business world. One of the first things we're taught as children is to say thank you.

We don't need to be thanking people for showing up each morning the way "modern parents" congratulate their children each morning for brushing their teeth or putting on their pants. The reality is that many of our teams expend a great deal of effort to meet goals within timelines. We work late, help colleagues, take on extra initiatives, navigate difficult meetings, call in for a critical client call while on vacation or on a day off. There are examples of these types of contributions weekly on most teams. Your "thank you" is really saying "I see you," "I appreciate your effort" and perhaps "I'm glad you're on the team."

Share successes

A client sends an email raving about their experience. The leadership team notes the contribution your team made to last month's results. The team lands a large deal. Strong leaders who foster trust are quick to share this praise with the team. People managers couldn't be effective without their team. Nothing says I appreciate you like publicly praising your team.

Early in my career I worked for a hard driving, entrepreneurial-minded organization. One year, we had a big hairy audacious goal to significantly grow our assets under administration. There were multiple strategies deployed and we were firing on all cylinders throughout the year. Turns out we hit that audacious target plus 5% that year. The team was elated. It feels good to win. At the next town hall the leadership team distributed some swag to commemorate the accomplishment. It's surprising how happy a pen or travel mug can make us. Then at the end the leader announced that they wanted to share the accomplishment with everyone. Everyone in the organization was given an extra day of vacation that year.

To be honest with you, I was elated with my travel mug. I didn't expect anything more. When the extra day was announced, you would have thought Oprah had just offered us all a new car. "You get a day off and you get a day off" (meant to be read in Oprah Winfrey's voice).

Over my career I've been fortunate enough to be awarded, as a gesture of appreciation and recognition, with certificates, awards, trips and shares. I've appreciated all of them. But the extra day off touched my heart and the memory has stuck with me. It was genuine and unexpected. It was a way of saying that we appreciate your effort in achieving this success. It was definitely a message that we are a team and we win together.

So, what's my point here? Is it to walk around with free vacation day certificates in your pocket? Of course not. You'll likely be popular but I'm not sure it will improve your trustworthiness. My point is that the most impactful acts of appreciation are the least expensive and often free. If I think about it, over the course of that year, the number of extra hours I had put in would have added up to multiple days of extra time so the one day off was technically free. But that wasn't the point. It was delivered by a leadership team that had already fostered high trust and the extra vacation day was perceived to be a sincere and generous act. The real cost of this gesture was the time and energy it took to decide they wanted to provide a meaningful gift and then make it happen.

Chapter 17: How Managers Can Foster Trust With Their Teams

Demonstrate vulnerability

Since Brene Brown's viral TedTalk in January 2011 and her subsequent books, the concept of vulnerability as a valuable leadership attribute has been widely adopted. But what exactly is vulnerability and how do we foster it as leaders? The best way to foster vulnerability is to model it for our teams. Let me share the story of Kyle and Kwame.

I worked with Kyle and he was always cool with me but he had a reputation, well-deserved, of being a bit of an asshole. On the surface, he embodied many of the attributes of a strong leader. He was bright, confident and well-spoken. He read all the right business books that just happened to be displayed on the bookshelf in his office. He attended the annual local TedTalk conference. He said all the right, progressive leadership slogans and phrases, but in reality, he was terribly insecure and known to undermine his colleagues.

When he heard about an issue on a colleague's team, he would never reach out to offer assistance personally. Instead, he would wait for an audience, probably a large meeting and then find a convenient and often awkward way to say something like, "I heard that internal audit found a number of deficiencies on your team. If there's anything me or my team can do to help you clean things up, just reach out. We really want to support you." I'm not even sure how one would respond to that. Do you say thank you? Two other words would pop into my mind first.

It turns out that Kyle is deeply insecure about his financial acumen. He's not in finance however in an executive role, the ability to quickly read and process financials is critical. It takes Kyle longer than his peers—too long in his mind—to read and process financial statements. The solution for him is to take a continuing education course at the local university to improve his skills in this area. This is commendable. The course requires him to be absent alternate Fridays to attend class. He's so insecure that he's sworn the handful of people who are aware of his course to secrecy. He saw this skill gap for him as a vulnerability. This was the type of thing he would choose to exploit in others and was a afraid to have his perceived weakness exposed.

His secret was leaked and several people knew and also knew it was top secret. The situation left Kyle looking insecure and weak which was precisely what he was trying to avoid.

Compare Kyle's attitude to Kwame's. Kwame assumed the role of head of operations at a pharmaceutical company after years in retail operations. Kwame was a charismatic leader with a strong track record for creating high performing teams and generating superior results. Quickly after taking on the role, Kwame had a town hall meeting with his entire new team. He introduced himself, shared how excited he was to work with the team and was very honest about his lack of pharmaceutical experience. After sharing the attributes and skills he is eager to bring to the team, he shared that he's on a learning curve about the industry and he'll rely on the team's expertise as he moves quickly to come up to speed.

Kwame's approach was the opposite of Kyle's. Why pretend that he had experience that he didn't? A quick search of LinkedIn would confirm his background. He was confident in the value he would bring to the team. Clearly the folks who hired him had confidence in him as well. By being vulnerable and open about what some would consider a gap, with his lack of pharmaceutical experience, he diffused the topic. In contrast to Kyle, Kwame came off as confident and capable.

Chapter 17: How Managers Can Foster Trust With Their Teams

Kwame made it okay for his team members to be transparent about their gaps and ask for help.

Embrace mistakes as learning opportunities

Who embraces failure? We read business books about the value of failure. We watch TedTalks about it. Ask any business person, when things are good, about their thoughts on failure and you will hear many logical, balanced and positive perspectives on the topic. They are all very hypothetical and inspirational.

But when the shit hits the fan and we screw up, we aren't thinking, "what doesn't kill me makes me stronger." We're thinking, "kill me please."

Failure is like Buckley's cough syrup. It tastes awful but it works to help us grow…..with one caveat: as long as we are smart enough to learn from it.

Hearing real stories from the trenches from real people we know is far more valuable than trite phrases and memes on social media.

But we don't share the stories of our epic failures. We push them out of sight for fear that they provide evidence that we are incompetent, irresponsible and likely not worthy of breathing the same air as all of our super-competent colleagues.

The time I didn't listen to my instincts

I recall a moment in my career I felt was an epic failure. It was one of my early people management roles. The team was expanding its scope and I had to hire a number of new team members. Eager to fill the roles and get the recruitment process behind me, I was a little hasty with one of my hires. The individual looked great on paper and passed all the due diligence checks. I made call to this potential team member's reference. The transcript of the call would have been a perfect reference check, but I sensed something. There was something in the tone of the reference that seemed curious. There was a little amusement at first in his voice as I explained I was calling for a reference. Clearly my candidate hadn't given him the heads up that someone may be calling. I picked up on a hint of insincerity. A sense of "sure, I'll give a reference." It seemed like he was the go-to person for any reference checks.

I will spare you the painful details and fast forward to 7 AM in the morning when I showed up at my boss' office after barely sleeping the night before. I had spent the previous day in meetings with HR and corporate security. My hasty new hire was about to be expediently exited from the organization that afternoon in a sting operation that would have seemed cool if I wasn't so demoralized that I made a bad hiring decision. I couldn't get over the fact that I didn't listen to my intuition and request a second reference. I thought the predicament I was in demonstrated poor judgment by me in my new people management role. I entered my boss' office looking like I lost my best friend, my puppy ran away, and my ice cream cone fell on the ground.

My boss at the time chose to share with me a few of his poor hiring decisions in the early years of his career. He was a great storyteller and within a few minutes we were both howling with laughter. He shared where he screwed up, what he learned and what he employs today to ensure those mistakes are never repeated. Then he got me to share how I think I could have

Chapter 17: How Managers Can Foster Trust With Their Teams

handled the situation differently. He agreed with my remedy and admonished me for being too hard myself, explaining that if I planned to manage people over the long term, I would make other mistakes and the value is to learn the lesson, shake it off and move on.

He modeled learning from mistakes and helped me to do so as well. It was a transformational discussion and I'm always ready to share my own missteps to help team members' process their own challenges and to remind them we all make mistakes. Learn from them, shake it off and move on.

Remember that we all have biases

This one is more challenging. The fact that we have biases is likely unconscious to us. One of the best books I've read on this topic is **Subliminal: How your unconscious mind rules your behaviour**, by Leonard Mlodinow, a theoretical physicist. Mlodinow outlines in his book that as much as we believe we are rational human beings who look for evidence then form logical conclusions based on that evidence, in reality we do the opposite. He said we typically have a belief and then we search out evidence to make us right.

Having a bias is human. We employ our biases to make snap conclusions about the world. The challenge is that by nature of being unconscious, we aren't aware of these programs running in the background. Where this becomes a problem is when these background biases are controlling our decision-making process and leading us to behave in a manner that disadvantages others.

Unconscious bias can be deadly when it shows up in policing in the form of racial profiling. Sadly, there is a long list of innocent people, including children, who were killed just because they were perceived to be threatening.

In the workplace it shows up in different ways like managers who always hire and promote individuals who look like themselves.

Our unconscience bias can create socially awkward encounters

I recall attending a holiday party and being seated at the table with my team members. One of my team members arrived, sat down and introduced me to his wife as "Dionne". His wife graciously shook my hand and asked me if I was one of her husband's team members. There were awkward stares from the other folks around the table. I responded to her politely that I was, in fact, her husband's boss. He was on my team. I can't know for sure why she assumed her husband was my manager. Perhaps because I was a Black woman and that was her immediate assumption. I'll never know but I suspect unconscious bias was behind her assumption.

In that scenario it was a matter of a few awkward moments, but it came up again in a more impactful scenario. When I was ready to go back out to work after having my first son, I started canvasing my network for a consulting contract. I met with one leader with whom I had mutual friends who had shared that I recently had a son. We had a great chat and caught up on each others' lives. She mentioned she needed some help on a project that would be a fit for however it was in a different city and having a young child at home, she didn't think I would be the best option. She didn't ask me, she made that decision. I

Chapter 17: How Managers Can Foster Trust With Their Teams

know she meant this to be supportive and empathetic to my life circumstances except that I am a grown adult and I am capable of making those decisions for myself. She didn't know if I may have been able to relocate for a few months and viewed that as a great adventure for me and my family. She was making decisions for me. That was the last time I was open about the fact that I had a young son. That ensured that any decisions to be made about the appropriateness of a role would be made by me, not by other people making assumptions about me based on their own life experiences.

We read about the missteps of large organizations that publish marketing material that is perceived by some groups to be insensitive and promoting negative stereotypes. It's shocking given the army of approvals typically needed to approve anything that gets shared with the public that no one catches them beforehand. Here are a few high profile examples:

Do you remember the H&M ad in 2018 featuring a Black boy wearing a sweatshirt with the words "coolest monkey in the jungle"?[4] There are historical examples of people of African descent being referred to as monkeys in a racially-motivated, derogatory context. As a result, this ad was quickly pulled after substantial consumer backlash.

What about Heineken's ad for its light beer where a bartender slides a bottle of its new light beer past 3 dark-skinned patrons to a white woman at the end of the bar with the tagline, "Sometimes lighter is better."[5] The racial undertone here and the overt statement that "lighter is better" seems blatant to me. Again, it's surprising no one caught this beforehand.

When I was a kid, companies like banks would produce an annual calendar that they distributed to clients each December. A number of times my family and I flipped through this calendar to discover there wasn't a single person of colour depicted in the 12 lifestyle images. It was always interpreted by me that people who looked like me weren't valuable clients so there was no need to include us in this fun, but symbolic calendar.

When the backlash comes in, the question in my mind is, "how did no one catch this before it made its way into the public domain?" Ads don't just get published publicly. Customer-facing material usually goes through extensive vetting by marketing, communications and legal just to list a few. A senior executive usually signs off on it as well. This marketing material somehow slips by all of these gatekeepers yet once it hits the public domain it becomes immediately clear that's it's culturally insensitive, racist or exclusionary.

These insensitive campaigns are deployed partly because there isn't a diversity of perspectives on these teams and bias prevailed.

There are excellent resources available to assist managers in building diverse teams and fostering inclusiveness. I would offer simply that in addition to building diverse teams, we actively seek out opposing perspectives. I confess that I am a fan of concurrence. I like to tick boxes and quickly move onto the next thing. When too many people are agreeing with us, we should be concerned. Where are the dissenting opinions? What's another way of looking at this? We may land on the same decision but it makes for a better solution when we've talked through potential alternatives.

Chapter 17: How Managers Can Foster Trust With Their Teams

Accommodate if you can

We discussed already that the purpose of our presence in the organization is to fulfill the organization's mandate and deliver value to our stakeholders. This is non-negotiable because if we can't do this to the best of our ability, we won't be around to accommodate anyone.

High work volume is a reality for many professionals. It is what it is. There is a profound difference, however, in working through a heavy workload with an inflexible manager who lacks empathy compared to a benevolent, yet demanding boss who treats you like an adult.

You know what you need to do. You also know that the plumber has a last-minute cancellation and can be at your home to look at the leak in your bathroom at 2:30PM this afternoon or two weeks from now as originally planned. Or maybe your daughter is performing her first vocal solo at her school's music concert on Thursday at 10 AM.

The concern I often hear is, if I accommodate one person, I'll need to accommodate everyone. Well, yeah. Why not? The situations where I've seen this as a problem is where you have a team member who is not conscientious with their work and would take advantage of the situation. But that's your issue, not the issue for your hard working, diligent team members who appreciate your flexibility in allowing them to navigate the many parts of their life and not feel as stressed. Less stress and worry about how they can make all the parts of their life work together means there's more energy available to be channeled into doing their best work.

The COVID-19 pandemic demonstrated to us that we can pivot quickly to alternative ways of working. Let's maintain an open mind, flexibility and adaptability about the options available to accommodate team members while continuing to produce quality work.

PART 3

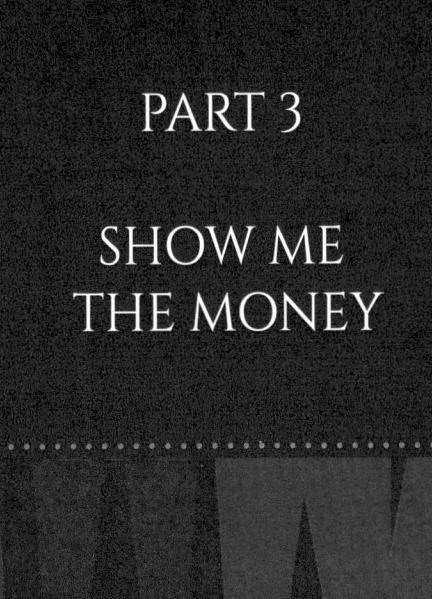

SHOW ME THE MONEY

Chapter 18:
How Trust Impacts the Bottom Line

It's unlikely that superior financials would be the primary driver for leaders to foster a high trust corporate culture. Frankly, there are much easier ways to produce strong financial results. I've already stated in chapter 5 (***Do organizations need to be high trust to be successful?***) that there are many low trust organizations that are producing decent profits without feeling any need to hold themselves accountable and making the hard choices that I describe in the high trust company profiles throughout this book. One thing will become clear as we look at the financial benefits of high trust organizations: low trust organizations pay what Stephen Covey calls a "low trust tax" in his book ***Speed of Trust.*** Costs are simply higher for low trust organizations. Let's take a look at how trust impacts a company's bottom line. Get ready, as the list of benefits for high trust organizations is quite long.

In their HBR article "The Connection Between Employee Trust and Financial Performance", authors Stephen Covey and Douglas Conant note, "trust is not a soft, social virtue — it's truly a hard, economic driver for every organization." And

Chapter 18: How Trust Impacts the Bottom Line

in their book **Smart Trust**, Covey and co-author Greg Link again refer to a "low trust tax" levied on low trust organizations. They go on to describe that when trust drops, speed goes down and costs go up. These cost increases are driven by the incremental actions that individuals decide to take to compensate for the lack of trust they have in the individuals they are doing business with whether it's their colleagues, their boss or a vendor. Perhaps more individuals are asked to engage in the decision-making process than is technically needed. More meetings are scheduled to hold individuals accountable to deliver what they promised. These extra steps slow things down.

Where can we find trust on a company's financial statements?

Trust doesn't have its own line on a company's profit and loss statement as I mentioned earlier in this book. Rather, it impacts most of the lines. Here's the lengthy list of financial benefits that high trust organizations enjoy:[1]

- Lower employee turnover
- Lower employee absenteeism, accidents and errors
- Greater propensity towards innovation, agility and fast decision making
- Higher client satisfaction rate
- Higher stock market returns
- Attract more high calibre talent
- Lower incidence of unions
- Improved sense of goodwill
- Higher energy levels, leading to doing our best work

Low trust organizations miss out on these benefits resulting in a higher cost of doing business which is their "low trust tax." Let's take a look at each category in more detail so we have a clear picture.

Higher Employee Engagement

In 2019 Gallup found that only 35% of employees surveyed in the US described themselves as engaged at work. This number is shocking as it's actually the highest the engagement rate has been since Gallup started to measure engagement in 2000.[2]

The level of employee engagement is an important metric that many organizations measure with different diagnostic tools. Employee engagement surveys are commonly deployed at least annually, sometimes more frequently. When your employees are engaged, there's a high likelihood they are both interested in and focused on doing their work which they find meaningful. It's also less likely they are online searching for a new job. High employee engagement generally means there's a high level of commitment and trust in the organization and employees feel their leaders set them up for success. Having a high trust organization directly and positively impacts employee engagement which is connected to all of the benefits we are discussing in this section.

Higher employee loyalty

The stats show that when employees trust and respect their leadership, they are more likely to stay with the organization. It

Chapter 18: How Trust Impacts the Bottom Line

turns out treating people fairly and setting them up for success provides you with good karma brownie points, allows you to sleep well at night and also fosters employee loyalty. Studies in 2016 show that the voluntary turnover rate, or the rate at which employees quit for other opportunities, was approximately 50% lower in high trust organizations compared to the average company's turnover rate.[3]

Employee turnover is a reality for any organization. People move to different cities, change industries and go back to school. People move to other organizations for job opportunities that aren't available within their current organization. This is just the nature of things.

The issue arises when your staff are leaving your organization because they can't stand management? They feel they are treated unfairly. They feel unsupported by their manager.

The cost of employee turnover is quoted as being anywhere from 90-200% of the employees' base salary.[4] Even the low end of that range is a staggering cost. Consider that turnover accounts on average for about 12% of pre-tax income for most organizations[5] and it becomes clear that it's financially prudent to ensure turnover remains as low as feasible.

Let's consider the costs associated with a high turnover rate

A vacant position represents a lost opportunity. An empty seat doesn't produce output. Additionally, the work doesn't disappear when there are vacancies. If you have a team of 12 people and there are regularly 2-3 vacant roles, it is likely that some activities are just not getting done and some activities are being handled by other team members who already have a full plate. Vacancies add stress for the other team members. It also lowers their productivity and makes it difficult for the team to be successful. It doesn't matter if you are part of a team in finance, sales or technology support, the reality is sales targets are missed, reports are late and internal or external clients are waiting excessively long for the support they need. Morale is eroded as a short-staffed team works harder to continue to come up short of their goals.

As a former people-manager, I am intimately familiar with what the recruitment process often looked like for me. When I needed to fill a vacant position, I didn't get a window of time when I can clear my desk of all other responsibilities and just focus on recruitment. Rather, recruitment becomes an additional task to be managed along with my existing full plate of responsibilities. Even when I had an effective and supportive human resources team doing the posting and initial filtering of potential candidates, as the manager, I still needed to review the short list of candidates and select whom I wanted to interview. Next I would prepare some good questions and dedicate time to the interviewing process.

Once the new candidate is chosen and they accept, there's rarely a turnkey comprehensive training program I can turn our new hire over to and have them return 2-3 weeks later fully trained. Rather, it's a combination of training programs, reviewing documents we provide, having them shadow team members and eventually they'll move up their learning curve to become a fully productive team member.[6]

Then there's a learning curve

This is the time it takes for an individual to become fully productive in their role. It can take anywhere from a few weeks to a year depending on the complexity of the role. There are

Chapter 18: How Trust Impacts the Bottom Line

a number of components involved in moving up the learning curve on a new job. There's the process and procedures which are the easier component of training. Process and procedures can usually be easily referenced using online manuals. Routine roles that perform standard processes repeatedly will have the shortest learning curve. With more complex roles, there is more than just the process to learn. It takes a while to understand something as simple as whom you reach out to for what. I need to send an internal communication to the organization. Who is the point person for that? Sure, there are organizational charts, but it's not always clear who the contact is for each question that comes up. Then, as the new hire builds trusting relationships, they are able to leverage these relationships to get their questions answered and get things done.

These trusted professional relationships are priceless for me. I can't count the number of times I've needed to rely on my relationship with a colleague to get something done. Sometimes shit happens. I recall once when a leader committed to having a communication out by the end of the month. The problem is, he forgot to tell me and it was 1:30 PM on March 31st. In this case, I was able to leverage the good relationship I had with the communications specialist to pull this off in what was about 4.5 days shorter than the normal turnaround time. We did it. The world wouldn't have ended if we didn't but we wanted to make an honest man out of the leader. It helps that I have a track record of always giving this communications specialist ample time for any requests so when the odd urgent request pops up, she usually accommodates me if she can.

In other situations, I screw up. I know you find it challenging to picture, but sometimes, despite my best efforts and organizational skills, I completely forget something. Wait. Its March

31st and I committed to getting a quarterly update out by the end of the month. The only thing left for me to do is turn on the charm, beg for help and hope there isn't another high priority that would make it impossible for this to happen today.

These scenarios are part of that learning curve. It takes time for a new hire to build this institutional knowledge and strong, trusting business relationships to allow them to expertly navigate the challenges that inevitably come up.

Considering all of these implications of having high turnover in your organizations, the projection that vacancies can cost up to 200% of an employee's annual salary begins to make sense.

When high trust organizations enjoy high employee retention, it means their managers aren't constantly splitting their time with interviewing and training staff, teams are not striving for success while chronically understaffed and they minimize the number of team members on their learning curve at any given point in time.

Absenteeism, Accidents and Errors

As we noted earlier in this chapter from the Gallup poll, only 35% of employees in the US report being engaged at work. In a study by Queens School of Business it showed that employees who were less engaged had 37% higher absenteeism rate, 49% more accidents on the job and errors and defects were up 60%.[7] Absenteeism, defects and accidents sounds like stats you would find on a human resources report but these issues have a tangible impact on your daily operations. Your employee satisfaction will be negatively affected and you'll have trouble attracting

Chapter 18: How Trust Impacts the Bottom Line

high quality team members. Clients will feel the impact and the company's reputation and brand will take a hit.

Absenteeism

Most of us have faced that Monday morning dilemma at least once. That's where our weekend ends far more abruptly that we had anticipated and we suddenly find ourselves frantically looking for our cell phone to snooze the alarm that is rudely interrupting the final hours of our sleep. How did Monday morning get here so quickly? I've heard some people experience this dilemma five days a week as they dread the time they spend at work. Absenteeism impacts a business in many ways. The most obvious way is that the absent employees work likely won't get done that day. Productivity goes down. If absenteeism is chronic throughout the organization, the impact can be far greater than an individual or team missing its goals.

Chronic absenteeism can result in having to maintain higher staffing levels than your high trust competitors to accommodate for the higher absenteeism rate. It may mean that you are paying out more overtime than expected to meet your production targets. Ultimately, our clients are often impacted by high absenteeism in an organization. Turnaround times aren't met. They need to wait longer than reasonable to speak to someone in your organization whether it's in your storefront or on hold waiting for someone in your contact centre.

Have you ever called an organization's contact centre to get a recording apologizing for the longer than usual wait times due to higher than expected call volumes? There are so many reasons that would lengthen wait times on any given day. Absenteeism is one reason. When I get that apology recording multiple times when I call a company I get frustrated and start thinking, do you have higher than expected call volumes or lower that required staffing levels?

My point is that high absenteeism rates will impact your client's experience.

Similar to employee turnover rates, there are expected absenteeism rates. People get sick or leave early for an appointment or let in the repair person to fix their air conditioner at home in the middle of a heat wave. Sometimes we need a personal day to take care of all the stuff that goes on in our lives outside of work. This is not what I'm referring to. I'm speaking of chronically high levels of absenteeism that is beyond the norms for your industry.

Accidents

Low trust organizations have a higher rate of on the job accidents. This is an issue on multiple levels. Most importantly it jeopardizes the health and well-being of team members. People get hurt or worse.

Beyond that major concern, it would also impact operations. Injured staff would be off. Working in an environment prone to accidents certainly doesn't help employee trust or engagement. It's a negative cycle.

It also would add to the rate of absenteeism and ultimately your voluntary turnover rate.

Errors

The higher incidence of errors has a few impacts. It impacts productivity as errors get caught in quality assurance and work has to be re-done. In some cases, a defective product may need to be thrown out increasing costs. If a defective product makes its way to your customer, customer satisfaction is eroded. Your

Chapter 18: How Trust Impacts the Bottom Line

brand could take a hit as you get a reputation for low quality products. Then, your productivity is impacted once again when your customer service channels are hit with increased calls or visits to fix, replace or return the defective product. Who wants to have a large group of employees engaged in activities just to handle defects? If you minimize errors and defects, you free up these staff members to deal with more high value activities and your customer satisfaction levels remain intact.

Innovation, Agility & Faster Decision-making

Innovation

Based on the 2016 Great Place to Work® Fortune 100 Best Companies to Work For Innovation Index, it shows that high trust environments foster many of the attributes that fuel an innovative culture. These attributes are:[8]

1. Embracing honest mistakes and failures as learning experiences to fuel future success. Employees need to feel safe to raise their hand and admit to mistakes.
2. Including employees in decision making where feasible
3. Encouraging high levels of cooperation and collaboration
4. Showing appreciation for team's extra efforts

Agility

"The Secret Formula for Organizational Agility" is a study conducted in 2014 by the Institute for Corporate Productivity, identified trust as one of the most impactful attributes a company can foster to drive agility.

Faster Decision-making

Faster decision-making and agility are inextricably linked. Making decisions is often one of the key road blocks to forward momentum on business initiatives and projects. One of the key attributes of high trust organizations as we outlined earlier is trusting that you will be treated fairly.[9]

Unlike low trust organizations that put a hit out for whomever was responsible for the last screw up, leaders in high trust organizations understand that failures and honest mistakes are the path to success as the team tests and learns what doesn't work on their way to designing a formula that does work. We're not talking about mistakes that occur as the result of sloppy work or lack of due diligence. We're talking about testing and learning and pushing the limits to improve products, processes and services.

When you know you're supported and will be treated fairly, you're more willing to make decisions faster knowing you can course correct if necessary. Failure isn't fatal in high trust organizations. There's also an acknowledgement that the extra time and work required to try to get to 100% certainty before making a decision is usually not worth the effort. An assessment is made of the worst-case scenario and people get comfortable pulling the trigger with 50% or 60% certainty. To be clear, for situations like launching humans into space or performing high risk brain surgery, the threshold for certainty is much higher. But most of us aren't involved in those types of life or death initiatives so trade off the level of certainty with the potential impact of a wrong decision and go with it.

In low trust workplaces it's more common for staff to feel they have responsibility without the corresponding authority to influence their work. If there's a lack of empowerment,

Chapter 18: How Trust Impacts the Bottom Line

most decisions need to be made at senior levels as others in the organization aren't trusted to make the "right" decision for the organization for even the simplest matters. In low trust organizations, there are typically layers of approvals required in what we affectionately refer to as bureaucracy, red tape and soul-sucking process. Professionals are often tied up on a daily basis with meetings and inundated with email. It can take several days to obtain the approval of multiple managers. We also need to factor in the turnaround time should they pose questions prior to being able to provide their approvals.

In low trust organizations, fresh ideas are often killed on the vine. Fresh ideas are new things that have never been tried before that may be amazingly successful or may blow up in my face and jeopardize my ability to remain in this role long enough to have a well-attended retirement party and start drawing my pension. Many a person would take their pension and party over a fancy new idea. New ideas are scary in low trust environments. When things go wrong and the leadership team needs a scapegoat, you want to be far away from that crime scene.

Higher client satisfaction rates

Higher client satisfaction rates are a natural consequence of all the items we covered above.

Lower turnover rate

You probably have a minimal number of vacant positions and most of your staff are fully trained. Trained staff provide better service and make fewer mistakes.

Low absenteeism

This means that your clients rarely call in and hear that you are experiencing longer wait times that normal. Requests are processed within stated guidelines and you're able to maintain competitive turnaround times.

Low incidence of errors

This means as a customer I will probably receive my product on time in working order. Without the added cost of re-work and defective products that need to be thrown out, you can maintain a competitive price.

Innovation, agility and fast decision-making

Innovation, agility and fast decision making results in competitive products, processes and turnaround times. Employees in high trust organizations also enjoy a higher level of empowerment than other organizations which means they don't need to escalate a client's request to seven managers to get an answer. High trust organizations want to push decision making authority down as low in the organizational structure as feasible and focus on the best possible client experience.

All of these factors lead to high client satisfaction rates and higher retention rates. But there's more.

Chapter 18: How Trust Impacts the Bottom Line

Stock market returns 2-3 times higher than average

In their HBR article *The Connection Between Employee Trust and Financial Performance*, Stephen Covey and Douglas Conant point out that two-thirds of the questions and criteria used in the annual "100 Best Companies to Work For" survey run by The Great Place to Work Institute along with Fortune, are focused on trust. This means that trust is one of the dominant characteristics that drive a company to be deemed one of the "best places to work". The companies on this list have annualized returns roughly three times that of the S&P 500 companies.[10]

Higher client retention rates, lower employee turnover, greater productivity, lower absenteeism, lower error rates and the other benefits have a direct link to dollars and cents on the company's profit and loss statement. By focusing on fostering a high trust organization, you're reducing costs and increasing the profit margin of each widget you sell.

Low trust organizations have three main issues in addition to running at a higher operating cost. Low trust organizations have the burden of additional costs for redundancy, compliance and politics.[11]

- Redundancy – there are many layers of management required to double check people's work and make sure rules are being followed. There is little empowerment so a lot of time is spent just requesting and waiting for the approval to do all kinds of routine activities. Low trust organizations don't trust their people to make prudent decisions.

- Compliance – in low trust organizations excessive documentation, rules and policies are required. Employees aren't trusted to do the right thing so we have to outline in a prescriptive manner exactly what you can and can't do. Now your management team needs to spend a fair amount of their time monitoring everyone to ensure they are complying with all of those rules and regulations. We have created an environment whereby we can't trust employees to complete their job without adult supervision.
- Politics – so much time is spent with unproductive side deals and hidden agendas that it wastes valuable time and money and frustrates us in the process.

If you're still unconvinced of the value of trust, let's add a few additional benefits:

Lower incidence of unions

If we consider the history of unions, they were introduced specifically to address the fact that historically, companies couldn't be trusted to treat their employees fairly. As such, employees organized and collectively engaged with company leadership to put rules and policies in place to essentially ensure that employees were treated fairly. They call that process collective bargaining.

Unions sometimes get a bad name for complicating the negotiation process, but they are credited with ensuring their workers get fair wages, benefits, reasonable working hours, etc. In many cases, these fair working conditions would never have been achieved without collective bargaining.

Chapter 18: How Trust Impacts the Bottom Line

With high trust organizations, employees don't fear being treated unfairly so there's no need to have a union as a negotiating body in the middle, between employees and management to make decisions. It's always more efficient when management and team members trust each other and can negotiate directly with each other and come to an agreement amicably and fairly.

Goodwill

Goodwill is always a good idea. I'll use the example from the earlier chapter ***Do you need to be high trust to be successful as an organization.*** I feel like a hostage to that company that I described in the chapter. I continue as a client because I don't have any viable alternatives. I am anxious for an alternative to show up as I will cancel my account with them as soon as it's humanly possible. There is no goodwill between us.

In contrast, I love my cell phone provider. They treat me in a manner that makes me believe that they value me as a client. Anytime I speak with their customer service team, which is infrequent as things run as I expect, it's always a productive conversation that usually resolves my issue or answers my question. I'm a long time client and have had a consistently positive experience with them. I recall seeing an ad for a service being offered by one of their competitors with a poor track record for customer service. I enthusiastically called my beloved cell phone provider assuming that they would have the same service. It turns out they didn't. My response was," no problem, I can live without it for now". I value their commitment to me as a client. There is goodwill between us.

Chapter 19:
Are you Trustworthy?

In the company profile section we share stories about the empowered, positive cultures found in organizations like Patagonia, Netflix, Salesforce and others. We hear these organizations have all kinds of cool things like experts coming in to coach staff on healthy living, encourage staff to get outside and surf over lunch or provide on site childcare. At Netflix the vacation policy is - when you need one - take one. We fantasize about these perks and wonder when our organization will adopt some of these enlightened practises.

If you were paying attention, you would have also noticed that these organizations are also rigorous in their recruitment practices. They hire trustworthy adults and they treat them like adults. They don't micromanage but rather trust the people they hire to do their jobs and to do what's in the best interest of the organization and its stakeholders. They hire adults who can handle the responsibility and accountability that comes with empowerment and autonomy.

If people act in a manner that demonstrates they can't be trusted, they are professionally yet expediently exited from the organization.

Chapter 19: Are you Trustworthy?

You see, you can't maintain such a high level of empowerment and trust when you have people on the team who are untrustwothy and primarily interested in how they can benefit themselves even if it's at the disadvantage of their co-workers, the organization and its clients.

I recall working at a particularly uninspiring organization shortly after university. I was a temp but the full-time staff got two "sick days" each month. At the end of each month there was a ritual where everyone would determine which two days they would be "sick" in the coming month.

I remember taking on an ambitious initiative to re-structure one of their filing systems. I was pumped and set an aggressive timeline of one month to complete the task. I recall a full-time staff member strongly suggesting that what I deemed to be a one month effort was more realistically 2-3 months effort. The message was clear. They wanted me to slow my roll and temper my enthusiasm. They weren't interested in having an eager beaver around. They didn't want me setting expectations management may want the rest of the team to meet. In this office, everyone was looking out for themselves, "taking care of #1". Of course this was a more complex dynamic with both management and the team driving that culture. Needless to say, I didn't stick around there very long.

My point is that maintaining a high trust organization is a reciprocal arrangement between the leadership and their employees. It is impossible to maintain a high trust work environment when there's a contingent of workers actively taking advantage of the empowerment and autonomy that is generously provided.

So while we fantasize about working in an organization that makes the investment to hire career coaches as part of the benefits package and install a hot yoga studio for stress relief, ask yourself if that company would want you as a member of their team. Are you a high trust employee that would appreciate the organization's investment in you and do your best work while protecting the best interest of the organization, its employees and its clients?

Chapter 20:
Who do you want to be?

I've shared stories, research, persuasive arguments and company profiles about the merits of being a trustworthy leader. As much as I would like to tell you that the only moral, ethical, civilized, intelligent and rational choice is to choose to be trustworthy, sadly, that's just not true. I would love to declare that unless you pursue a path of trustworthiness you'll wind up destitute and depressed. Again, not true. There are individuals and corporations who fit solidly in the category of untrustworthy yet they appear to be thriving by all external measures.

Being trustworthy is a personal choice

Trustworthiness comes down to the question, "who do you want to be?"

We can't explore trustworthiness without dipping our toes in the murky waters of politics. It's almost expected that politicians won't follow through on their promises. The only mystery is which ones will be kept versus those that will be abandoned, never to be discussed again like the cabbage soup diet. Politicians routinely backtrack on statements, contradict themselves and some blatantly lie. Many of those same politicians enjoy financial success and power.

Let's consider US Senator Mitch McConnell, the longest tenured US senator who was initially elected in 1985. McConnell has served on many influential committees and senior roles in government including the Majority Party leader. Politics is a polarizing topic and Mitch has a polarizing personality. His supporters love him and consistently elect him to office, allowing him to maintain his seat over the past 3 decades. There's another camp of people who can't stand him. This group is primarily made up of his political opponents and some media outlets.

One of the most blatant acts of hypocrisy pertains to his position on replacing Supreme Court justices in an election year. The Supreme Court is the highest court in the US and justices receive lifetime appointments. The Supreme Court is a key opportunity for the ruling party to make a lasting impact on the country. Although laws that govern the country originate from the government, it's the courts and its judges who influence the interpretation of those laws and determine how those laws will play out in the daily lives of Americans. When a President has the opportunity to appoint a Supreme Court judge, it's a unique and impactful opportunity to ensure they place a justice on the Supreme Court who will interpret laws in alignment with the ruling party's ideology. This ensures that the current ruling party can influence how laws will be interpreted long after their party is out of power. This is why Supreme Court judge appointments are coveted opportunities for Presidents to shape the future of the country.

The Supreme Court judge Antonin Scalia passed away in February of 2016 with the next presidential election scheduled for November of that year. McConnell adamantly stated that because it was nine months to the next election, "The American

Chapter 20: Who do you want to be?

people should have a voice in the selection of their next Supreme Court justice. Therefore, this vacancy should not be filled until we have a new president." He successfully blocked the approval of a replacement for Justice Scalia. He further clarified that his position to advise his colleagues not to approve a replacement for Justice Scalia was "about a principle, not a person."

Fast-forward a short four years later to 2020 and we have a more extreme scenario. Beloved Supreme Court Justice Ruth Bader Ginsberg (RBG) passed away in September of 2020, just two months prior to the next presidential election. This was the identical scenario that presented itself in 2016 with a Supreme Court vacancy opening up in the year of a presidential election. The only difference was that in 2016 when McConnell claimed it wouldn't be right to fill the position until the new President was elected, the election was 9 months away and in 2020 the gap between RBG's death and the presidential election was 7 weeks.

McConnell did a 180 degree turn on his own words and alleged principles and rushed his party to replace RBG within the 7 weeks prior to the election to ensure they could nominate a candidate that reflected their party's core values.

This could be seen as political strategy. The only way that I interpret it is hypocrisy and a clear indication that McConnell's principles and core values are flexible and shaped by whatever is in his best interest in the moment.

In the world of politics, Mitch McConnell is not unique in playing fast and loose with integrity. What differentiates McConnell is how incredibly skilled he is at it.

Let's get back to the original question, "who do you want to be?"

From the outside looking in, McConnell seems like a successful and fulfilled human being living the life he wants. I think he probably sleeps well at night. He's one of the wealthiest and most powerful Senators. For many people, McConnell is "winning" however I wouldn't trust him, "as far as I could throw him."

Let's take this into an organizational context

Let's go back in time to March 14, 1989. That's the day that an Exxon oil tanker collided with the Bligh Reef and subsequently spilled 11 million gallons of oil into the Alaskan waters known as the Exxon Valdez oil spill.

Over thirty years later, this area has yet to recover from the devastating environmental, economic and social impact of the spill. The oil spill resulted in the death of over 100,000 seabirds, over 3,000 animals including otters, seals, eagles and orcas. The loss of 26,000 tourism jobs and $2.4 billion in business.[1] The social impacts have been researched and uncover the types of impacts that are typically related to high unemployment. The destruction of the local fisheries industry destabilized local families as parents had to leave to seek employment in other areas. There was also a reported increase in the level of alcoholism in the community.

Despite triggering an environmental disaster whose effects would still be felt over thirty years later and the settlements that Exxon would have to pay, *The Washington Post* (April 3 1989) stated it would have a minimal impact on Exxon's overall financial results.

Upon investigation, it became clear that the leadership team at Exxon knowingly flouted regulatory guidelines and safety measures. The Exxon Valdez was running with less staff than required, creating a situation where staff would be tired from having to work longer hours than deemed safe. The collision

Chapter 20: Who do you want to be?

detection system on the vessel had been broken for over a year, a fact that was known to the management team at Exxon.

Exxon spent over $2 billion in the cleanup effort, however the company also engaged in some behaviour that makes us question Exxon's integrity.

Exxon executives went on a lawsuit spree.

Exxon filed a lawsuit against the captain of the ship, claiming that he was intoxicated the night of the collision. The captain was, in fact, drunk that evening but he was also off-duty. The judge significantly reduced damages levied against the captain in that lawsuit.

Exxon also filed a lawsuit against the state of Alaska claiming they negatively impacted the cleanup effort by delaying the approval to use chemicals in the cleanup.

Exxon then filed a suit against the Coast Guard. The simplest way I can explain this lawsuit is that Exxon basically said, you granted us permission to sail in those waters so aren't you ultimately responsible for the collision and subsequent oil spill?

One of the most questionable actions taken by Exxon was to sign a secret financial settlement with a group of area seafood producers for $63 million on the agreement that the seafood producers would repay any future damages that may be awarded to them. The seafood producers agreed not realizing that upon settlement of the lawsuits that were in progress, they would have been eligible for more like $750 million in damages. Exxon also kept this settlement quiet during their main lawsuit prompting the judge to call them out on this distrustful behavior.

Exxon was initially ordered to pay $5 billion in damages which was reduced to $507 million through multiple appeals.

The livlihood of countless Alaskans including indigenous communities and wildlife were permanently affected by this environmental disaster. Exxon, however, continues to be a thriving business. Sure, if you Google "Exxon", this oil spill will invariably pop up in the results. The situation is studied in university classrooms around the world as a cautionary tale of what not to do.

My point here is that, despite this being a cash outlay for the company and really bad press, Exxon continues to thrive as a company. Even the shipping vessel got a new lease on life. After a makeover it was relocated to another part of the world and renamed the Exxon Mediterranean.

What was Exxon's response? They produced a video with a favourable portrayal of their role in the cleanup. Critics were vocal that the facts on record contradicted most of the content of that video.

I share these stories to illustrate the unfortunate truth that choosing to be trustworthy isn't the only path to riches and power if that's what you're looking for. It's a personal choice.

We get to choose who we want to be in the world. It has nothing to do with what the folks around us are doing. It definitely has nothing to do with doing what's easy. I'm sure by this point in the book it's clear that choosing trustworthiness can often be the more challenging road in the short term.

Dave Chappelle chose who he wants to be

I think Dave Chappelle's story illustrates what it means to intentionally choose who you want to be.

Dave is wise, brilliant, hilarious, sometimes controversial and always true to who he is and what he believes. In 2004 his comedy show *The Chappelle Show* was wildly popular. His fame was on an upward trajectory as he would sell out huge

Chapter 20: Who do you want to be?

stadiums for his stand up concerts. Based on the interview Dave provided for David Letterman *My Next Guest* on Netflix, Dave grew increasingly uncomfortable during this period. He speaks about an incident that happened while he was taping a skit on race, one of Dave's hot topics. One of the crew members laughed at the wrong moment, which made Dave feel uncomfortable. Was the message getting across? Were people laughing with him or at him? Additionally, Dave was moving through life in the fast lane with little time for self-care. He had no time to build meaningful relationships with his children. Dave describes that he loved being famous but disliked celebrity.

In piecing together Dave's comments about this period, it sounds like he felt uncomfortable with the state of his art. He wondered if his satire being received in the spirit that it was intended. Overall it sounds like he felt a little out of control, like the tail was wagging the dog. He was the dog and the entertainment industry was the tail.

So he did what very few people would have the courage to do. In 2005 he walked away from *The Chapelle Show* leaving a $50 million contract on the table and moved to South Africa where he could hear himself think and figure out his next step. One of my favourite Dave quotes is "the idea of being courageous is that even though you are scared, you just do the right thing anyway." It wasn't easy. There were potential law suits associated with his departure. But he did it anyway.

Today Dave is back. He has built a life he loves in a small town in Ohio and is in full control of his career. Consequently, he's also at the height of his popularity. He chose who he wanted to be.

Who do you want to be? Is being trustworthy important to you? If the business decisions you make on a daily basis were published in the paper, would you be comfortable with that?

Trust can take a lifetime to build and can disappear in seconds. Trust me.

Thanks so much for reading.
I hope you enjoyed this book.
It was so much fun to write.
I have more books coming.
Use the QR code below to get added to the list
to **receive book release updates** and
get **access to book previews**.

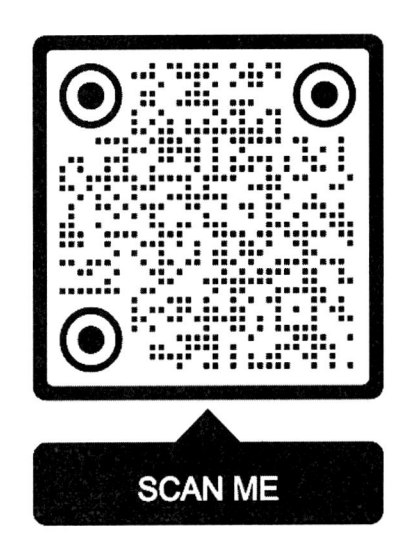

Endnotes

Foreward: Trust, Air and Celery

1. https://nationalpost.com/life/food/celery-expensive-medical-medium-celery-juice

Chapter 2 – Trust Doesn't Get the Respect it Deserves

1. https://www.bbc.com/news/business-34324772 - :~:text=In%20September%2C%20the%20Environmental%20Protection%20Agency%20%28EPA%29%20found,since%20admitted%20cheating%20emissions%20tests%20in%20the%20US.
2. https://www.nytimes.com/2015/09/21/business/a-huge-overnight-increase-in-a-drugs-price-raises-protests.html
3. https://www.washingtonpost.com/transportation/2019/04/09/doctor-who-was-dragged-screaming-united-airlines-flight-finally-breaks-silence/
4. https://www.forbes.com/sites/jackkelly/2020/02/24/wells-fargo-forced-to-pay-3-billion-for-the-banks-fake-account-scandal/?sh=76a8087542d2
5. https://www.washingtonpost.com/technology/2019/08/29/even-after-ubers-ipo-long-shadow-deleteuber-still-looms/
6. https://www.bbc.com/news/world-us-canada-55009228

Chapter 3 - High Trust Company Profile – Starbucks

1. "Onward: How Starbucks Fought For its Life without losing its Soul", by Howard Schultz, pg. 9-10
2. starbucks.com
3. https://www.statista.com/statistics/250166/market-share-of-major-us-coffee-shops/
4. https://www.nytimes.com/2018/04/15/us/starbucks-philadelphia-black-men-arrest.html
5. https://www.forbes.com/sites/roddwagner/2018/06/01/the-philadelphia-incident-was-terrible-starbucks-response-was-admirable/?sh=6f4aa98123bc

6. https://www.forbes.com/sites/simonmainwaring/2021/07/07/purpose-at-work-how-starbucks-scales-impact-by-listening-to-all-the-stakeholders-in-our-shared-future/?sh=74264fd35bfc

7. https://www.forbes.com/sites/simonmainwaring/2021/07/07/purpose-at-work-how-starbucks-scales-impact-by-listening-to-all-the-stakeholders-in-our-shared-future/?sh=74264fd35bfc

8. https://money.cnn.com/2010/06/07/news/companies/starbucks_schultz_healthcare.fortune/index.htm

Chapter 4 – It's the How not the What

1. https://www.goodreads.com/quotes/1324527-a-smooth-sea-never-made-a-skilled-sailor#:~:text=Quote%20by%20Franklin%20D.,never%20made%20a%20skilled%20sailor.%E2%80%9D

Chapter 5 - High Trust Company Profile – Zappos!

1. https://www.inc.com/magazine/20100601/why-i-sold-zappos.html
2. https://www.hcamag.com/ca/specialization/benefits/should-you-pay-your-employees-to-quit/242167
3. https://www.businessinsider.com/zappos-sneaky-strategy-for-hiring-the-best-people-2015-12
4. https://hbr.org/2010/07/how-i-did-it-zapposs-ceo-on-going-to-extremes-for-customers
5. "Delivering Happiness: A path to Profits, Passion and Purpose", by Tony Hsieh pg. 191-197

Chapter 7 - High Trust Company Profile – Berkshire Hathaway

1. https://www.marketwatch.com/story/trust-is-the-secret-sauce-in-companies-that-warren-buffett-and-others-value-highly-2020-12-17
2. https://fortune.com/company/berkshire-hathaway/fortune500/
3. https://www.volarisgroup.com/blog/article/trust-the-building-block-to-berkshire-hathaways-success
4. https://www.theguardian.com/business/2011/apr/30/warren-buffett-big-mistake-david-sokol-lubrizol

5   https://www.finn.agency/warren-buffett-reputation-berkshire-hathaway

Chapter 9 - High Trust Company Profile – Method

1   https://www.forbes.com/sites/alejandrocremades/2019/01/27/how-this-entrepreneur-went-from-zero-to-100-million-a-year-in-sales-within-24-months-of-launching/?sh=177460db4b29

2   "The Method Method: Seven Obsessions That Helped our Scrappy Start-up Turn and Industry Upside Down", by Eric Ryan, Adam Lowry and Lucas Conley, pg 31

Chapter 10 – What about creating Shareholder Value?

1   A Friedman doctrine-- The Social Responsibility Of Business Is to Increase Its Profits - The New York Times (nytimes.com)

2   https://www.goodreads.com/quotes/70385-the-purpose-of-business-is-to-create-and-keep-a

3   purpose.businessroundtable.org

4   https://www.ft.com/content/294ff1f2-0f27-11de-ba10-0000779fd2ac

Chapter 11 - High Trust Company Profile – Netflix

1   https://www.bloomberg.com/news/newsletters/2021-04-18/netflix-is-losing-market-share-but-is-it-losing-customers

2   Netflix culture deck (slideshare.net)

3   https://hbr.org/2014/01/how-netflix-reinvented-hr

4   https://hbr.org/2014/01/how-netflix-reinvented-hr

5   https://hbr.org/2014/01/how-netflix-reinvented-hr

Chapter 12 – Principles over Profits

1   CNN Health - Elizabeth Landau, CNN - Updated 11:04 AM EST, Wed February 5, 2014

2   Forbes, by Robert Glazier, April 2020, "CVS lost $2B with one decision. Here's why they were right"

3   Jennifer Riel and Roger Martin, special to The Globe and Mail, published October 13, 2017

4   https://www.theglobeandmail.com/report-on-business/careers/management/how-unilever-won-over-shareholders-with-its-long-term-approach/article36538572/

5   https://www.theglobeandmail.com/report-on-business/careers/management/how-unilever-won-over-shareholders-with-its-long-term-approach/article36538572/

6   NPR Nov 25 2020 https://www.npr.org/2020/11/25/938922031/netflix-removes-chappelles-show-at-dave-chappelles-request

7   Reuters April 17, 2017 https://www.reuters.com/article/us-american-airlines-results-idUSKBN17T1S6

8   Reuters April 17, 2017 https://www.reuters.com/article/us-american-airlines-results-idUSKBN17T1S6

9   "The Infinite Game", by Simon Sinek, pg 207

10 https://www.bloomberg.com/news/articles/2013-06-06/costco-ceo-craig-jelinek-leads-the-cheapest-happiest-company-in-the-world

11 "Miss Americana" Netflix

12 https://abcnews.go.com/US/colin-kaepernick-announces-million-donation-part-plan-protest/story?id=41822972

13 https://www.nytimes.com/2019/03/21/sports/colin-kaepernick-nfl-settlement.html

Chapter 13 - High Trust Company Profile – Patagonia

1   Patagonia's New CEO Plans to Keeping Up Climate Fight at Clothing Brand - Bloomberghttps://www.washingtonpost.com/business/a-company-that-profits-as-it-pampers-workers/2014/10/22/d3321b34-4818-11e4-b72e-d60a9229cc10_story.html

2   https://www.inc.com/scott-mautz/how-can-patagonia-have-only-4-percent-worker-turnover-hint-they-pay-activist-employees-bail.html

3   https://www.businessinsider.com/patagonia-mission-environmentalism-good-for-business-2018-12

4   https://www.patagonia.ca/one-percent-for-the-planet.html

5 https://wornwear.patagonia.com/

Chapter 14 - What Trust Is Not

1 NYT https://www.nytimes.com/2009/01/09/business/worldbusiness/09iht-jobs.4.19232394.html

2 NYT https://www.nytimes.com/2009/07/31/business/31pay.html

3 https://www.bbc.com/news/technology-46618582

Chapter 15 - High Trust Company Profile – Salesforce

1 https://www.statista.com/statistics/972598/crm-applications-vendors-market-share-worldwide/

2 https://www.inc.com/marcel-schwantes/what-salesforce-does-for-their-employees-that-make-other-companies-jealous.html

Chapter 17 – How Managers Can Foster Trust with their Teams

1 HBR: "Proven Ways to Earn Your Employees' Trust" by Carolyn O'Hara

2 "Extreme Ownership" by Jocko Willink and Leif Babin, pg 255 - 262

3 "The Power of Giving Away Power", Matthew Barzun - Chapter 5 – pages 103-135

4 https://www.washingtonpost.com/news/arts-and-entertainment/wp/2018/01/19/hm-faced-backlash-over-its-monkey-sweatshirt-ad-it-isnt-the-companys-only-controversy/

5 https://www.washingtonpost.com/news/arts-and-entertainment/wp/2018/01/19/hm-faced-backlash-over-its-monkey-sweatshirt-ad-it-isnt-the-companys-only-controversy/

Chapter 18 – How does Trust Impact the Bottom Line?

1 https://www.greatplacetowork.ca/images/reports/Business_Case_for_High_Trust_Culture.pdf

2 https://www.gallup.com/workplace/284180/factors-driving-record-high-employee-engagement.aspx#:~:text=Gallup%20found%20that%20in%202019,tracking%20the%20metric%20in%202000.

3 https://www.greatplacetowork.ca/images/reports/Business_Case_for_High_Trust_Culture.pdf

4 https://www.greatplacetowork.ca/images/reports/Business_Case_for_High_Trust_Culture.pdf

5 https://www.greatplacetowork.ca/images/reports/Business_Case_for_High_Trust_Culture.pdf

6 http://learn.greatplacetowork.com/rs/520-AOO-982/images/GPTW-Fortune-100Best-Report-2016.pdf

7 https://hbr.org/2015/12/proof-that-positive-work-cultures-are-more-productive

8 https://www.greatplacetowork.ca/images/reports/Business_Case_for_High_Trust_Culture.pdf

9 https://www.greatplacetowork.ca/images/reports/Business_Case_for_High_Trust_Culture.pdf

10 https://hbr.org/2016/07/the-connection-between-employee-trust-and-financial-performance

11 https://blog.employerscouncil.org/2018/10/15/the-high-cost-of-low-trust-cultures/

Chapter 20 – Who do you want to be?

1 https://www.history.com/topics/1980s/exxon-valdez-oil-spill

About the Author

Dionne England is a published Author, Business Consultant and workshop Facilitator located in Toronto, Ontario Canada. Dionne's literature focuses on her unique perspective on doing our best work and leadership for professionals within organizations. She brings her decades of experience in the corporate world to provide pragmatic and effective solutions. She challenges mainstream perspectives and connects on a raw level with her readers by continually delivering thought-provoking reading experiences flavoured with her irreverent humour.

Dionne loves working with managers to help them to lean into self-awareness, adjust their mindset, set productive boundaries, lower their stress level while delivering even better business results.

Dionne has her MBA from the Rotman School of Management at the University of Toronto.

Dionne can be contacted for consulting, workshops and speaking at contact@dionnethewriter.com.